ITALIAN 20TH CENTURY MUSIC

THE QUEST FOR MODERNITY

ITALIAN

MICHAEL D. WEBB

20TH CENTURY MUSIC

THE QUEST FOR MODERNITY

KAHN & AVERILL, LONDON

First published in 2008 by Kahn & Averill
9 Harrington Road, London SW7 3ES

ISBN 978 187108289 0

The author would like to thank the following for their permission to reproduce photographs
Archivio Edizioni Suvini Zerboni, Milan for pp. 27 (Alfano), 33, 68, 74, 79, 82, 93, 99,
101, 104, 115, 121, 136; Bideri postcards, Naples for p.27 (Tosti); Fondo Maderna, Bologna
for p.51; Fondo Pratella, Biblioteca comunale, Lugo for pp. 40, 41; Giovanna Marini for
kindly supplying the photo on p.77; Cristina Moregola for p.124; Roberto Masotti for p.135;
Sugarmusic, Milan for p. 111.

Set in 11 pt Joanna. Designed by Simon Stern

Printed in Great Britain by
Halstan & Co Ltd, Amersham, Bucks

CONTENTS

PREFACE

The idea of writing a book about 20th century Italian music first came to me in the late 1980s during my visits to Lugo, a small market town deep in the heart of the Romagnola countryside. I already knew that the town had musical connections. Arcangelo Corelli was born in a nearby village and his family are still landowners in the area. Almost two centuries later a certain Giuseppe Rossini returned to his native town with his wife and it was there, in all probability, that their son, Gioachino, was conceived though not born.

But the town's links with the modern era came more as a surprise. The discovery of a small museum dedicated to Pietro Mascagni in Bagnara di Romagna left me astonished and more than a little puzzled. I subsequently consulted all the books I had on the composer, but found no mention of his frequent visits to Romagna. However, on visiting the museum accompanied by its curator, the local parish priest, I discovered a vast collection of documents, including ample correspondence between Mascagni and a certain Anna Lolli, his secret country lover. My initial excitement was somewhat quelled when the priest informed me that only a few days before my visit an 'American journalist' had come to the museum and had made copious photo-copies of the most interesting material. My dreams of registering a 'scoop' sadly vanished.

Later, in January 1996, my imagination was further fired by a revival of Francesco Pratella's *L'aviatore Drò* at the Teatro Rossini in the centre of Lugo, the theatre where it had first been performed in 1920. Lugo had apparently been a regular meeting place for members of the Futurist movement, including the poet and founder of the movement Filippo Marinetti, the composer/painter Luigi Russolo and the critic Alceo Toni, who was also born in the town. I soon discovered that the composer's home, where these meetings had probably taken place, was on the same road as that of my future mother-in-law. Unfortunately, though, it had been converted into a car showroom and has only recently been given its full recognition.

Slowly but surely I began to piece together the turbulent history of Italian music at the beginning of the century. And it was at this point that I suddenly realised that here was a whole new world just waiting to be discovered, a world that had not even been hinted at during my musical studies in Britain. Why, I asked myself, should so much attention be given to the likes of Elgar, Bliss or even Vaughan-Williams, and so little to their Italian counterparts Martucci, Ghedini, Malipiero etc.? And how were forward-thinking composers like Casella, Dallapiccola and others affected by the twenty years of fascist rule that shaped the cultural life of mid-20th century Italy? I found some answers, but not all, in the existing literature on the period. But by now I was keen to link the beginning of the century to the end, a path that took me through the Darmstadt school, post-serialism and finally post-modernism. The name of Luciano Berio had obviously not been new to me, but I knew little or nothing of Bruno Maderna, Luigi Nono or Franco Donatoni, three names that dominated the musical thought of the postwar years.

During my research I came across a fascinating book that helped me draw many of the pieces together. Goffredo Petrassi, whose wonderful Concertos for Orchestra are now thankfully coming back into the international repertoire, had the dubious fortune of living right through the 20th century, making him the perfect witness to all the various artistic movements and events that had begun to stir my imagination. In 1991 an *Autoritratto* (or self-portrait) was published, the result of conversations with the composer cleverly put together by Carla Vasio, and here I found many of the missing pieces that I had been looking for. Petrassi not only speaks about his musical experience, but also paints a vivid picture of the cultural life in Rome during the first half of the 20th century.

By the 1990s Petrassi had already stopped composing due to his failing eye-sight. I nevertheless took the liberty of writing him a letter to congratulate him on his book and to ask his opinion about my intentions to write a book that would cover many people he had known or worked with. Some weeks later, much to my surprise and joy, I received a short reply. Modestly, or perhaps diplomatically, he told me that he was in no position to suggest which composers should, or should not be included in such a book, but that there were many authorative musicologists living in Bologna whom I should approach. And this is exactly what I did.

Although Bologna is no longer the innovative town it used to be (Wagner's *Lohengrin* and *Tannhäuser* were both given their Italian premières at the Teatro Comunale), it nevertheless has many interesting links with the music of the modern era. Respighi was born here, M.E.Bossi and Donatoni taught here and the Maderna Archives are housed in its ancient University. It was also the arena for Toscanini's notorious clash with the fascist authorities, an episode that precipitated the conductor's decision not to work in Italy until the régime had fallen.

I soon made contact with various musicologists living and working in Bologna who were only too pleased to share their knowledge with me. In the meantime I gradually became more familiar with the repertory by spending literally hundreds of hours listening, not unwillingly, to the third programme of the Italian national radio (Rai-Tre). Here I was able not only to hear the music, but I also had the opportunity to follow interviews and discussions that often involved the very composers I was writing about. Occasionally my research was further aided by the discovery of recordings on CDs accompanying specialist music magazines, many of which were, alas, on sale at half price due to lack of interest on the part of the general public.

Acknowledgements

My exploration of the fascinating but neglected story of Italian music in the 20th century would have been much duller without the help of a small but select group of contacts and friends. I am particularly indebted to the following people:

Mario Baroni, musicologist and former lecturer at Bologna University; Anna Rita Addessi, lecturer at Bologna University and expert in postmodern music; Alessandro Savasta and Gabriele Bonomo of Edizioni Suvini Zerboni in Milan; Bob Reeves, former director of music at the CCAT in Cambridge; Marina Milani, friend and willing interlocutor; and last but not least Maurizio Ascari, fellow writer and endless font of enthusiasm.

BOLOGNA, FEBRUARY 2007

INTRODUCTION

Italian 20th century music can, like the Italians themselves, be prone to extremes. The burning passion for the new so often encountered in a country that produced some of the greatest creative minds of all times is inevitably matched by an underlying, almost stubborn, sense of conservatism, a reluctance to deviate from what is safe and familiar.

Despite the long series of dramatic events that assailed Italy over the course of the twentieth century – the assassination of their king in 1900, the horrors of the First World War and the sweeping cultural changes that followed, two decades of fascism, the Second World War and the subsequent 'invasion' of American culture, the banishment of their last ruling king, the historic student riots of the 1960s and '70s and the myriad of political and social reforms that ensued – despite all this the Italians have remained their same high-spirited, inventive and fundamentally conservative selves.

And so it was that after a century of fervent attempts at musical reform and innovation, the most celebrated and best known form of 'modern' Italian music continued to be the much loved (and occasionally despised) Italian melodrama. With the help of homesick and nostalgic emigrants the popular genre was able to conquer the New World as well as the Old. And any thought of change was made even more difficult by Mussolini's virtual 'adoption' of the most established writers of *opera lirica* as the official representatives of Italian music during his 20-year régime.

The stereotype was destined to persist long after the end of the Second World War. Whose 'fault' this is remains a matter of debate and it was certainly not for the want of trying. The change in direction undertaken by many Italian composers after the fall of the fascist régime was, in fact, nothing less than radical. In little more than fifty years the overt sentimentality of Leoncavallo had been replaced by the daunting political intellectualism of Luigi Nono: a drastic move away from a style that aimed to please the masses at all costs, to one where the artist's personal expression was paramount and the whims of the general public were no longer pampered to.

This courageous – and some might say excessive – shift away from direct communication was redressed to a certain extent towards the end of the century, when the new generation of composers began to react against the harshness and complexity of much post-serial writing. But the general lack of interest in the non-operatic repertory was set to continue. Just how ingrained this attitude was can be evinced from the fact that right until the end of the century the Italian government insisted on subsidizing opera at the expense of other forms of music. In 1985, 42% of the newly established FUS (Fondo Unico per lo Spettacolo) was allocated to the so-called Enti Lirici. Almost twenty years later, when the new milennium had already begun, this amount was raised to 60%.

The enduring popularity of *opera lirica* and the difficulties and lack of recognition suffered by many composers of non-operatic music is just one of the various recurring themes of this brief but hopefully comprehensive survey. Another issue that clearly emerges is the enormous and sometimes underestimated influence that Verdi played on subsequent generations.

Before writing this book I had never actually realised just how influential a figure Verdi had been in shaping the character of Italian music in the 20th century. Not only did he definitively break with the tradition of set pieces in his later operas, a slow process that had started as far back as Bellini, but he also instigated a reappraisal of the wealth of Italian music written so many centuries before. It is largely thanks to Verdi, and to a handful of dedicated conductors, composers and musicologists, that the music of the Italian Renaissance and Baroque (Palestrina, Monteverdi, Vivaldi, Corelli and many others) which we now take for granted, was virtually rediscovered.

Verdi conveniently died in 1901, and in so doing provided me with a well defined starting point for my account. The first chapter of my book therefore deals with the last great period of Italian lyric opera, culminating in the triumph of the school of *verismo* (championed by Mascagni and taken to its extremes by Puccini). But I have also tried to provide sufficient background information to underline that the cultural and artistic life of a nation is inextricably caught up with the historical, economic and political situation of the time.

Chapters two and three pay homage to the few composers who, at the start of the century, were brave enough to move away from the stereotyped idea of Italian music. These include a group of musicians who attempted to break with the past by taking up the somewhat bizarre cause of Futurism. Unfortunately, the quality of Futurist music never came anywhere near to that of the vibrant works of art produced by the Futurist painters. It goes without saying that names like Pratella and Russolo have virtually disappeared from today's concert programmes.

These two chapters inevitably contain many names that will be quite unknown to most readers. I do feel, however, that their obscurity is no reason for their neglect. The vast majority of these early twentieth century composers deserve, in my opinion, just as much attention as many of the regularly recorded and performed composers of the same period from other countries. My only hope is that by writing about the likes of Martucci, Sgambati and Sinigaglia I will stir the curiosity of enough people to create a long overdue revival of at least some of the musicians in question.

A notable exception is, of course, Ottorino Respighi, whose three symphonic poems, collectively known as the Roman Trilogy, show no signs of disappearing from catalogues and concert halls. Like many of his contemporaries Respighi lived and worked through the so-called

ventennio of fascism and to some extent conformed to the requirements of the régime, especially in his later works. Chapter four takes
a closer look at the effect of this tragic yet fascinating period. Details
are given of the Italian musicians who suffered directly at the hands
of the régime and of the dramatic events that led to Toscanini's depar-
ture for the USA.

And yet, although the composers, writers and artists of the period all faced restrictions to their creative freedom, this never really
amounted to full-blown censorship (at least as far as music is concerned) and the importance of excellence was still recognised by the
authorities, if only to promote the image of Italy abroad. As a result
there seems to have been some tolerance in the face of modern ideas
and this minimum of flexibility allowed some of the more daring
composers to toy with such novelties as dodecaphony and serialism
in general. Chapter five illustrates how, despite the severe political
climate, the first signs of 'modernity' were already creeping into the
music of Dallapiccola and his contemporaries during the late 1930s.

The jubilant years immediately following the end of the Second
World War were largely dominated by the summer courses for 'new
music' held in Darmstadt (which were also attended by Stockhausen,
Boulez, Cage etc). The Italian contingent played a fundamental role
in the direction of the course and composers such as Nono, Maderna
and Berio were held in particularly high esteem. Their main achievements – above all their ground-breaking experiments in electronic
music – are outlined in Chapter six.

The 1960s and '70s heralded a period of cultural turmoil throughout the western world and student protests and riots in Italy disrupted
the everyday running of the country. The ensuing political and, above
all, cultural reforms meant that the somewhat exclusive, or at least
ethereal, nature of Italian music was no longer appropriate or accept-
able. Chapter seven describes how popular idioms and jazz began to
infiltrate the works of even the most 'serious' of composers. Mean-
while, the rapid advances in technology meant that live electronics
was fast replacing pre-recorded studio electronics during performances of modern music. The chapter also traces the slow decline of

the unbending dogmatism that characterised the original Darmstadt group and shows how many composers now began to experiment with a freer form of musical expression. This was not always easy, especially for younger composers who felt themselves to be under the stern gaze of their elders. Fabio Vacchi, for example, has often commented on how, in the early years of his career, he found the old avant-garde quite 'spaventoso' (literally 'frightening').

By the close of the 20th century the air had generally cleared and the adhesion or not to a particular faction or school of thought was no longer a source of polemics. Italy continued to produce a wealth of talented musicians and composers, despite the relatively little support coming from the state. Many, however, chose to live or at least work abroad, mainly in France but also in other European capitals such as Berlin – a situation, as I have pointed out in the conclusion of Chapter eight, very reminiscent of the early years of the 20th century when the most forward-thinking Italian composers found a more suitable climate for their innovations outside of their own country.

The criteria I adopted when deciding whether or not to include a composer in this book was basically a question of dates. If they were alive during part or all of the century in question then they qualified for possible inclusion. In certain cases this may only be a matter of a few years and in the case of Verdi barely two, but some of them played such an important role in laying down the foundations of what was destined to change the face of Italian music that it would have been impossible not to mention them. Needless to say, my major difficulty was in selecting representative composers from the end of the period in question and I sincerely apologise to anyone who feels that he or she has been unduly neglected.

Composers like Busoni and Menotti who spent most or a great deal of their lives abroad are amply covered in the book, but I decided not to include foreign musicians who took up residency and made their home in Italy. The most notable of this latter category is probably Roman Vlad, a Romanian musician and critic who witnessed at first hand the exciting developments that took place after the Second World War and whose writings and analyses undoubtedly provide a valuable basis for any study of the period. Hopefully the important contribution of such foreign artists to the development of modern music in Italy will be given full recognition elsewhere.

In conclusion, I feel I cannot overemphasize just how much my personal musical experience was enriched during the course of my research for this book. My exploration of modern Italian music led me to discover a whole new world of fascinating works that I had never been aware of: Setaccioli's *Sonata per clarinetto*, Busoni's *Berceuse Elégiaque*, Malipiero's *Quartetti per archi*, Pilati's *Sonata per flauto*, Ghedini's *Concerto dell'Albatro*, Petrassi's *Concerti per orchestra*, Maderna's *Ages*, Scelsi's *Uaxuctum*, to mention but a few. It is my heartfelt wish that after reading this brief account of what is largely unknown or abandoned territory, many other people, scholars and amateurs alike, will be prompted to share my enthusiasm for these and the countless other works that are waiting to be rediscovered.

THE TWILIGHT OF ITALIAN MELODRAMA

In 1909 Ferruccio Busoni wrote a curiously prophetic letter to his wife: "... It is election time and the whole of Italy is in a state of excitement ... whatever the result, the country will not change ..."[1]

As a potential innovator destined to be ostracized in Italy due to his Germanic connections, Busoni knew only too well that it was not merely a question of politics. The twentieth century was, in fact, to witness many brave efforts to 'modernize' Italian music, but, as we shall see, these were largely thwarted by a collective conservatism that did very little to assist the cause of artistic or cultural renewal.

At the turn of the century Italy was very much an agriculturally based country with much of its population, at that time around 40 million, working in and around the land.[2] From a cultural point of view it had an extremely rich patrimony to draw on and academically, too, the country had much to be proud of. But as a nation it was still in its infancy, barely 40 years having passed since the historical act of unification. The defeat of the Bourbons in the south and the eventual withdrawal of the Austrians in the north had left the country temporarily cut off from the rest of continental Europe and this meant that

1/ Busoni – Letters to his Wife (Edward Arnold & Co. London, 1938)

2/ Italy's eventual transformation into an industrial and service-based society was dramatic. By the end of the century only around 3% of the total workforce would be employed in agriculture.

by the end of the 19th century the Italians were more than a little wary of new ideas, especially when they happened to come from abroad.

It would be wrong, of course, to suggest that the *fin de siècle* restlessness that was sweeping through much of Europe, carrying with it all the good and bad that progress implies, was to leave Italy totally unscathed. Already at the end of the 19th century industrialisation was beginning to leave its mark on northern cities like Milan and Turin. The rapid spread of new factories meant that the working classes, as in the rest of Europe, felt an increasing need to protect their rights. In 1892 the Italian socialist party was formed and some years later, in 1898, riots broke out in several major cities leading to the death of a large number of workers. The slaughter was soon to be vindicated with the assassination of King Umberto I in 1900 at the hands of an anarchist who had apparently returned from the USA especially for the purpose.

But the lust for revolution was little reflected in the musical affairs of the country. During the last decades of the 19th century most of the younger generation of composers were well aware of the exciting developments taking place elsewhere and were eager to show how 'modern' they were by incorporating elements of French or German innovations into their works. Yet they often came up against a wall of resistance that can only partially be explained by political obstructionism. By far their biggest obstacle lay in the type of audience they were writing for.

Apart from a handful of courageous writers of European-style instrumental music, the Italian musical scene had for decades been overwhelmingly dominated by opera and in particular by that special brand of musical drama known as *opera lirica*. Although the most important opera houses were now being increasingly frequented by the new middle classes (who now rubbed shoulders with the minor nobility that had until then made up the bulk of the opera-going public), there was no guarantee that such an audience would take kindly to any form of innovation. The vast major of opera-goers went to places like La Scala in Milan or to the Regio in Turin to be seen and not necessarily to listen. They were understandably outraged by Arturo Toscanini's insistence towards the end of the 19th century that all the lights in the auditorium should be dimmed throughout performances.

Paradoxically, the greatest lovers of Italian opera at the time were probably the very people that were excluded from the theatres either on account of the high cost of tickets, or else due to the inaccessibility of the city to country folk. There are many accounts of how large groups of the less wealthy citizens would routinely gather outside opera-houses during performances or rehearsals in the hope of catching the latest melodies of their favourite composers or hearing the voice of the most fashionable singers.

In reality those who lived and worked in the country were not so isolated as one might think, for they enjoyed the benefit of 'second-hand' performances given by amateur companies on the occasion of country markets and fairs. It was nothing to hear farm-labourers whistling a familiar aria by Verdi or Donizetti as they worked the land and they often named their children after the most popular operatic characters of the time (Otello, Norma etc.).

It was against this background that Giuseppe Verdi (1813-1901) had begun his quiet, almost unwitting revolution. Although he never really stopped writing memorable and 'catchy' melodies that could be sung by farm-labourers or broadcast on barrel-organs, his greatest achievements are to be found at a somewhat deeper level, namely within the internal organisation of the works themselves. As his style developed and reached its glorious maturity, what remained of such time-worn conventions as set pieces and recitative were progressively streamlined and eventually eradicated. In his last and arguably greatest operas, *Otello* (1887) and *Falstaff* (1893), nearly all the traditional formal divisions have disappeared, the result being a well-balanced and virtually uninterrupted interplay between melody and declamation. At the same time the orchestra was finally liberated from its subordinate role as an accompaniment to the vocal gymnastics of the singers and began to take on a life of its own, enhancing and commenting on the action taking place on stage. Notable, too, is the literary polish of his later librettos, born of a happy collaboration between Verdi and the writer/musician Arrigo Boito (1842-1918).

Curiously it was Boito himself who had formerly been among the loudest voices accusing Verdi of being old-fashioned. And there was, at least on the surface, plenty of evidence to support this accusation. Verdi displayed very little desire to take part actively in any sort of revolution, musical or otherwise, and his attitude towards Wagner, the epitome of progressive thought at the time, was one of general disinterest. After attending the first Italian performance of *Lohengrin* in 1871 he commented that he had found it long and tedious.

Although the two composers could actually be said to have more than a few things in common, any attempt to compare Verdi with Wagner would at the time have caused little less than an uproar in some circles, since Verdi was very much seen as the great protecting father of Italian music, defending his recently unified nation against the onslaughts of foreign (and above all Germanic) invaders. And his famous dictum 'Look back to move forward' was indeed a heart-felt appeal for young musicians to take note of the historic achievements of Palestrina and other illustrious Italian masters of the Renaissance and Baroque whose music had long been neglected. By ending *Falstaff*, his very last opera, with an energetic fugue Verdi was surely leaving behind him a clear message for his younger compatriots.

It would take some time for this message to sink in, especially as far as opera was concerned, but the wide-ranging structural reforms carried out by Verdi had much more immediate effects. The new generation of Italian composers now felt at liberty to write operas without any of the artificial restraints that would inevitably have slowed down the pace of many of the action-packed 'thrillers' written during the 1890s and the first years of the 1900s. Even before the close of the century certain French and German idioms were timidly creeping into their music, but after the death of Verdi the floodgates were finally opened.

Perhaps the most serious attempts at assimilating Wagner's grand design were made by a small group of enthusiasts, which included Antonio Smareglia (1854-1929), Alberto Franchetti (1860-1942),

Italo Montemezzi (1875-1952) and Vittorio Gnecchi (1876-1954)[1], all of whom had a short but significant moment of glory during the first decade of the new century. And yet, despite the championship of Arturo Toscanini, a devoted admirer of Verdi but also a staunch Wagnerite, their works slowly disappeared from the programmes and by the end of the 20th century had been almost totally forgotten.

The most accomplished of the group was probably Alberto Franchetti. In 1902 Toscanini's first performance of *Germania*, probably the composer's most representative opera, was highly praised and subsequently met with wide international acclaim. The fruits of Franchetti's studies abroad are particularly apparent in this work and his elaborate orchestral writing together with an astute theatrical sense and love of special effects soon led him to become known as the 'Italian Meyerbeer'. Yet the flavour of the music, like that of most of his fellow Wagnerites, remains essentially Italian thanks to a pervading and unmistakable propensity towards lyricism.

At the end of the 19th century the international popularity of Italian melodic song was, in fact. at its height. Among the most celebrated Italian exports of the time were the song writers Paolo Tosti (1846-1916) and Luigi Denza (1846-1922), both of whom spent much time abroad, notably in Britain, where in 1908 Tosti was knighted for his services to the realm. Between them they wrote almost 1,000 'canzonette', many of which are still so familiar that they are often mistakenly attributed to some distant Italian folklore. Denza's evergreen *Funiculì, funiculà* was actually written as recently as 1880 to celebrate the inauguration of the funicular railway in Naples. It is no surprise, then, that the majority of contemporary opera writers were influenced, either directly or indirectly, by this hugely successful fashion.

The problem of reconciling this outstanding gift for melody, a national trademark that not even Verdi had renounced, with the demands of Wagner's 'through-composition' or the use of the leitmotif

1/ Vittorio Gnecchi's standing was considerably enhanced when in 1907 Richard Strauss was accused of borrowing from the Italian composer's opera *Cassandra* (1905) to use in *Elektra* (1909)

was no small matter. Composers such as Pietro Mascagni (1863-1945), Ruggero Leoncavallo (1858-1919), Giacomo Puccini (1858-1824), Umberto Giordano (1867-1948)[1] and to a certain extent also Francesco Cilea (1866-1950), tried to resolve the issue by making only passing reference to any such Wagnerian traits and unashamedly allowed melodrama and pleasing melodic arias to pervade their operas. Giordano's alleged comment that the formula for success consisted of finding a good song and writing an opera around it probably sums up the prevailing spirit of those years. Moreover, the success of this formula, which did much to nurture the development of that particular brand of Italian opera known as 'verismo', was further aided by a growing sense of national pride among the general Italian public. As a result it was the latter faction and not the more progressive Franchetti and colleagues that in the end survived the test of time.

The term 'verismo' is not an easy concept to define. Generally speaking the plots of the operas in question moved away from the historical themes used by Verdi, but at the same time avoided the mythological idealism characterising the works of Wagner. Composers sought to bring their operas up-to-date by dealing with contemporary themes, preferably tinged with an element of dramatic violence aimed at capturing the attention of the audience. Such effects may have shocked the prude, but they certainly delighted a large part of a new bourgeois public who were thirsting for scandal and sensationalism. While the essence of literary verism, rooted in the novels of French writers such as Zola, was fairly successfully captured by Italian writers including Verga and Capuana, the musical counterpart, inspired in particular by Bizet's *Carmen*, tended to be much more superficial and the overriding importance given to lyrical melody make the movement a purely Italian affair.

In 1890 the first performance of what has come to represent the quintessence of Italian verismo, Mascagni's *Cavalleria Rusticana*, turned its composer into a national hero overnight. This one act opera, based

---

1/ Giordano displayed a brief but memorable flare for experimentation in his highly successful opera *Siberia* (1903), where the instrumentation includes, among other things, the prototype of a 'prepared' piano and a colourful balalaika band.

on a book by Verga, is a typical tale of passion, violence and the mal-treatment of an innocent heroine. It is hard to imagine the scale of popularity Mascagni achieved on the merit of a single work, a success by no means confined to the borders of Italy. During a trip to Buenos Aires in 1911, more than 20 years after the launch of the opera, he claimed to have been mobbed on arrival by the local Italian commu-nity, who, in his own words, "tore my clothes, bruised my arms and chest ... and wrecked my car".

Mascagni has suffered a great deal of criticism over the years, not so much for his music, but rather for his extravagant behaviour. His self-assured character doubtlessly helped to promote his work in a ruthless and business-like manner, something which, all things con-sidered, is only to be admired. But his inability to accept criticism often led him to argue and break off important friendships with the likes of Puccini and Toscanini, only to make up with them again after years of ill-feeling. On top of all this, his dubious relationship with Mussolini and the Fascist movement, yet to be clarified, certainly did not help his reputation in certain circles.

From a musical point of view Mascagni tried very hard to get away from the tag of being the 'composer of the *Cavalleria*', but never re-ally succeeded. To call him "an egocentric muddler out of his depth"[1] is, perhaps, a little too harsh, but his cause was certainly not helped by the interview he gave to the newspaper *Il Corriere della Sera* in 1911 where he declared: "When I run out of inspiration I'll start writing symphonies". The fact that, apart from some youthful sketches, he left us with no symphonic music would lead us to the conclusion that his font of ideas never really dried up.

While Mascagni seems frequently to have made a conscious effort to experiment with new ideas, there is in reality little evidence of any genuine stylistic development during his long career. His later operas, for example *Isabeau* (1911) or *Parisina* (1913), might contain some interesting harmonic progressions, but they certainly can not be called innovative. What is more, like many of his works they suf-

---

1/ John Rosselli: *Music & Musicians in nineteenth-century Italy* (Amadeus Press 1991).

fer from the fact that he invariably wrote his music at the piano and then hurriedly transcribed it for the orchestra, more often than not to meet impending deadlines.

Very different was the case of Giacomo Puccini. Of all the verist composers a special place should be reserved for this much loved and much discussed figure, for he alone succeeded in developing an idiom which was unmistakably his own. Even if the German musicologist Adorno once dismissed him as a composer of 'light music', Puccini should at least be granted the merit of going out of his way to keep in touch with the very latest developments in European music. Having absorbed all he needed from Wagner and Massenet he began to look elsewhere and was soon attracted to the exotic world of Claude Debussy. His fascination for the French composer's experiments in orchestral colour resulted in a new lightness and transparency in the orchestral scores of operas like *La Fanciulla del West* (1910), while the many references to the orient in later works are an indisputable testimony to his awareness of what was happening outside of Italy and more especially in France. And his dabbling with new harmonic solutions in the early years of the new century became so marked as to attract the attention of none other than Arnold Schoenberg, who, in 1911, cited Puccini's work in his landmark treatise Harmonielehre.

In reality, though, Puccini was never destined to extend his musical idiom much beyond that of the late romantics and any search for the influence of Stravinksy's *Rite of Spring* or Schoenberg's *Pierrot Lunaire*, two contemporary compositions which are known to have attracted his curiosity, will inevitably be in vain. Even the influence of Debussy never really extended to any real experimentation. The Italian public was, in any case, far from being ready for ventures into such territory. The fact that the first Italian performance of Debussy's *Pelléas et Mélisande* in 1907 had been disturbed by members of the audience lamenting its lack of melody could not have made it easy for an established Italian composer to consider writing anything in the way of a truly 'modern' opera.

And so it was that easily digested melody – later to be defined by some critics as 'melodia stanca' (tired melody) – continued to be the staple diet of concertgoers in Italy. As late as 1917 Puccini was still adopting time-honoured formulas to conclude arias like 'Dimmi che vuoi seguirmi' from Act 3 of *La Rondine*, with the melody rising to a triumphal climax in the final phrase and then descending gently towards the cadence, a 'show-stopping' technique frequently adopted in Italian popular music.

To be fair to the composer it should be said that he was fully aware of such banalities. He did apparently try to eliminate another such aria, 'Parigi! È la città dei desideri', from *La Rondine*, realising that it would interrupt the dramatic flow of the story, but due to the insistence of the general public it was, and still is, included in most performances of the opera. The only time when Puccini seems to have attempted a stand against the tyranny of public taste was in the three one-act operas which make up the so-called *Trittico* and more notably in the first of the series, *Il Tabarro* (1918).

Nowadays, when listening to certain passages from this fascinating and to some extent atypical work – the repeated evocation of the movement of the River Seine, the dark and foreboding Cloak theme or the twisting chromatic colouring of expressions referring to drunkenness – we realise that Puccini may have been desperately trying to catch up with his times. Here the use of the wholetone scale at last makes sense, being symbolic and not merely ornamental, while the introduction of a motorhorn in the score could even be linked to the ideals of the Italian Futurists. And although the work still contains its fair share of melodrama, the lack, for example, of memorable arias shows how he appears to be avoiding some of the clichés that had brought him fame. Not surprisingly, though, such a non-lyrical opera proved to be one of his most unpopular and Toscanini's unkind comments about the work led to one of the numerous rifts between the two musicians.

His final opera *Turandot* (1924-26) shows a clear return to the characteristic sweeping melodies much loved by Puccini's fans. But the fable-like storyline that makes up the plot is a far cry from the true-to-life dramas of his earlier works and as such the label *verismo* begins to lose its significance. On top of this there are also signs that he was at last trying to update certain other aspects of his musical language. During his last years Puccini is said to have taken a great interest in the music of his compatriot Casella, at that time one of the most adventurous Italians of the new generation. But despite all good intentions the more original touches – strange harmonic progressions, the presence of a second orchestra on stage, the use of an enormous chorus hidden behind grotesque masks – that are often referred to as marking out *Turandot* from the rest of his operas are in the end little more than 'special effects'.

Incidentally, the story of the completion of *Turandot* merits a certain attention. Although Puccini's publishers Ricordi consulted the authoritative Toscanini before making any decisions, the choice of Franco Alfano (1875-1954) to carry out the conclusion of the final act was not so automatic. The conductor's preferred candidate is actually said to have been Zandonai, but his idea was rejected, apparently on the grounds that the composer's own operatic idiom was already too well developed to be able to write in the style of Puccini. Zandonai's case was naturally not helped by his frequent and overt attacks on the policies of the publishing house in question. And so the task fell to Alfano, a well-established composer of a wide range of vocal and instrumental music who is now remembered almost exclusively for his completion of another composer's opera.[1]

Alfano was in fact a talented writer of operas in his own right and in some ways could be said to have succeeded in crossing the bridge at which Puccini had faltered. As early as 1904 when he completed *Risurrezione*, his first critically acclaimed opera, it was clear that he was attempting to create a work that was not overdependent on musical effects and melody. Not surprisingly, the greater part of the work was written while he was visiting Paris and Russia, where he presumably felt freer to follow his own inclinations rather than being subject to any restraints that the Italian public may have imposed. The fruits of his travels abroad are, however, probably best seen in what is gener-

---

1/Alfano's one claim to fame has recently been jeopardised by Luciano Berio's alternative version of the conclusion of *Turandot* (see Chapter 7).

Paolo Tosti   Franco Alfano

ally considered to be his most important work, *Sakùntala* (1921), a three-act opera based on an ancient oriental fable. Here the influence of Debussy, notably that of *Pélleas et Mélisande*, is felt not only in the harmonies and instrumentation[2], but also in the high level of integration between text and music.

The other candidate for the completion of Puccini's *Turandot*, Riccardo Zandonai (1883-1944), is also worthy of mention in that he too was able to bridge the gap between the patrimony of the 19th century and the challenge of the twentieth century, something his teacher Mascagni had desperately wished to do without ever really succeeding. Of his seven operas probably the most significant is *Francesca da Rimini* (1914), a medieval tale based on a play by D'Annuzio. The transparent score of this work suggests an awareness of the new approach to instrumentation that was being developed outside of Italy,

2/ Unfortunately the original score was destroyed during the Second World War and the opera had to be reorchestrated by the composer while already in his mid-seventies.

while the inclusion of such 'ancient' instruments as the lute and the viola pomposa together with the subtle use of ancient modes points to a renewed interest in a musical tradition long forgotten by Italian musicians. The result is an opera with a freshness that relieves the listener from the monotony of Giordano or the excesses of Wagner.

Such a tendency to look back to beyond the 19th century was becoming increasingly common among younger composers attempting to escape from the stranglehold of the stereotype into which Italian opera had fallen. In many ways Verdi himself seems to have sensed this need for a change of direction when he wrote *Falstaff*, a comic opera harking back, in theme at least, to Mozart's *Così Fan Tutti* or *Le Nozze di Figaro*. And to give Mascagni his fair due, already before the turn of the century he had been considering a work based on a comedy by the 18th century Venetian writer Goldoni. This eventually led to the composition of *Le Maschere* (1901) and although he seems to have had Rossini in mind when conceiving the opera rather than any more truly classical model, Mascagni was nevertheless one of the first of the new wave of Italian composers to draw inspiration from the traditional *Commedia dell'arte*.

The trend becomes even more apparent in the works of Ermanno Wolf-Ferrari (1876-1948), a composer with the dubious advantage of having a mixed Italian-German parentage, or, more to the point, Venetian-German. After the success of the classically inspired *Il Segreto di Susanna* (1909), which owes much in concept to Mozartian opera, he began to look towards Venice, the city of his birth, for inspiration. This path inevitably led him to take up Mascagni's lead and turn to the most celebrated of Venetian playwrights, Goldoni. He went on to write five operas based on the plays of Goldoni, the most well known of which being *I Quattro Rusteghi* (1906), a light-hearted work suffused with simple folklike rhythms and melodies set against a delicate orchestration.

Like so many of his generation, though, Wolf-Ferrari's musical style failed to develop much beyond a basically 19th century idiom. As late as 1935, when he wrote his last Goldonian opera *Il Campiello*, he was still writing in a prevalently diatonic idiom, with only a token use of ancient modes and folk melodies. From a historical point of view his importance lies not so much in his musical achievements, but rather in his confirmation of the growing respect for the past.

Similar comments could just as easily be made about many other composers of Wolf-Ferrari's time, who tried hard to move away from the clichés of *verismo* but never quite made it. The works of Riccardo Pick-Mangiagalli (1882-1949), for instance, were, like those of Wolf-Ferrari, often inspired by the *Commedia dell'Arte*, but in his search for modernity he never looked much further afield than Wagner and Strauss; he thus became caught up in the time warp that seems to have entrapped so many Italians during the first decades of the twentieth century.

Finally, we come to the unusual case of Lorenzo Perosi (1887-1956), a composer who may well have turned out to be a prolific writer of opera had his calling as a priest not prevented him from venturing into the dubious world of the theatre. In the circumstances he put much of his creative energy into the writing of another vocal form, the oratorio. His sudden and rapid rise to fame recalls that of Mascagni, depending as it did on a single piece which met with a clamorous overnight success. The work in question, the cantata *In coena domini* was first performed at a catholic congress in Venice in 1897 and was shortly afterwards transformed into the larger-scale *Passione Secondo S.Marco*.

Spurred on by this unexpected success Perosi went on to write a considerable number of liturgical settings using an idiom where the Italian passion for melody is combined with chromatic harmonies and an overtly Wagnerian orchestration. While his music has much in common with that of the Verismo school, recognition is due to Perosi for being one of the first composers to really take notice of Verdi's admonishments. It should not be forgotten that Verdi's last work was not an opera but rather the religiously inspired *Quattro Pezzi Sacri* (1886-1897). And it is equally no surprise that Perosi's passionate interest in fugue and above all in polyphony, best seen in his more modest masses and motets, soon led him to be hailed as the new Palestrina. No other composer had, until then, dedicated themselves with such energy and devotion to the study of the liturgical music of the Baroque and Renaissance.

To pinpoint the exact moment when the decline of *verismo* began to set in would be a difficult task, for even though the Fascist movement's virtual adoption of the opera lirica as their official model probably extended the life of certain *verismo* operas (see Chapter 4) by at least a decade beyond their natural expiry date, certain leading figures of the school seem of their own accord to have grown wise with the passing of time. Giordano is a case in point. After years of enormous popularity (almost exclusively based on works written at the end of the previous century), he finally admitted that with the composition of his last opera *Il Re* (1929) it was time to conclude a chapter in the history of Italian music.

This did not necessarily mean that opera had become obsolete as an art form – even the most outspoken critics of *verismo*, notably Casella and Pizzetti, wrote a fair number of operas between them. The Italian melodrama had nevertheless fallen into a state of stereotypy and the moment had arrived to come to terms with the enormous changes that had been taking place in the rest of Europe during the first two decades of the 20th century.

2

PIONEERS AND REVOLUTIONARIES

Long before Mascagni had been struggling to find a new musical language more suited to the challenges of the modern world he saw opening up around him, other Italians had already been busy preparing the way for what they believed to be music of the future.

This was no easy task since, as we saw in the previous chapter, the Italian musical scene at the end of the 19th century was largely dominated by a collective obsession with opera and above all with melody. And while it is true that concerts of purely instrumental works were slowly becoming more popular, thanks to the growing number of Quartet Societies and the so-called 'people's concerts' in Turin, programmes still tended to contain a large amount of operatic or pseudo-operatic material in the form of overtures, preludes, interludes and transcriptions. Entire symphonies were rarely performed and even then were usually 'cushioned' by lighter pieces in order to make the evening's menu more palatable.

This seemingly obstinate refusal of anything that came from across the Italian border (in this case the fundamentally German concept of the symphony) had in reality a certain historical justification. For almost a hundred years the Italians had been invaded or dominated by various foreign powers and it was no surprise that after their hard-won unification much of the population had been left with a bitter taste in their mouths.

The earliest attempts by more internationally-minded composers such as Franco Faccio (1840-1891) to write large-scale symphonies had not met with any great or lasting success, but this does not mean that an Italian brand of instrumental music did not exist. Many composers now known exclusively for their operas did, at some point, also try their hand at instrumental music. Even Puccini, whose non-operatic output was admittedly not vast, wrote several small-scale instrumental works including a youthful *Preludio sinfonico* for orchestra (1876) and an elegy for string quartet called *Crisantemi* (1890), which was very popular at the turn of the century and is still occasionally performed or recorded more than 100 years later[1]. But while such works are not displeasing to the ear the fact remains that from a developmental point of view they were at least 30 years behind their times and did little to contribute to the cause of modernisation taken up by other more ardent reformers.

And yet despite this fundamentally unfavourable climate two of the most important pioneers in the resurrection of purely instrumental music managed to make a name for themselves without writing a single opera. The first of these, Giovanni Sgambati (1841-1914), had the advantage of being exposed to a wider European environment than most of his contemporaries. Although he was born in Rome he was almost entirely brought up by his English mother, who was determined to give her son a broader musical education than was customary in Italy at that time. He also had the good fortune of studying the piano with none other than Franz Liszt, who was resident in Rome during the 1860s, as well as having the honour of being befriended and encouraged by Wagner in the 1870s.

Sgambati was first and foremost a concert pianist and spent much of his life touring the capital cities of Europe, where he came into contact with a wide variety of musical styles. A great deal of his music was naturally written for his own instrument, but he also composed several interesting pieces for chamber groups and even for full orchestra. From a historical point of view, his importance lies principally in his efforts to Europeanise Italian music and to familiarize the Italian public with the works of composers 'from across the Alps'

---

1 / The piece appeared, for example, in the programme of a chamber concert given during the 2001 Salzburg festival.

(among other things, he conducted the first Italian performance of Beethoven's Eroica Symphony).

The second great pioneer, Giuseppe Martucci (1856-1909), likewise wrote no operas. He nevertheless spent much time and effort promoting both Italian and foreign opera and in 1888 made history by conducting the first performance in his country of Wagner's *Tristan und Isolde*, a work considered outrageously progressive for the time. His output as a composer was, though, strictly limited to purely instrumental music and a number of his orchestral pieces remained in the repertory, both at home and abroad, long into the 20th century. His two symphonies (1895, 1904) are rare examples of full-scale romantic works written by an Italian at the turn of the century. The influence of the German school is, of course, unmistakable, and the works display a skilful blend of the austerity of Brahms and the flamboyancy of Wagner. Another outstanding work, the haunting *Canzone di Ricordi* (a song-cycle originally composed for voice and piano 1886-87 and later orchestrated), could even be said to rival similar works being conceived at that time by Mahler.

Giuseppe Martucci

But despite the pervading Mittel-European flavour, a distinct Italian element remains in the music of Martucci. During the first decade of the 20th century he set about orchestrating many of his earlier piano pieces and it is here that we clearly understand that his heart and soul were still in his country of origin. In what is probably his most popular concert piece, the *Notturno* (op.70, no1, orchestrated 1908), the tradition of sweeping Italian melody is dominant throughout, despite the lush instrumentation. And his Neapolitan origins are more than apparent in the light-hearted and familiar *Tarantella* (op.44, no 6, orchestrated 1909). Toscanini, a great upholder of the Italian patrimony, held the composer in such high esteem that in 1931 he agreed to organise and conduct two commemorative concerts in his honour, which, as we shall see later, turned out to be a historical event in more sense than one.

Apart from Sgambati and Martucci only a handful of other composers completed Italy's offering to full-blown European romanticism in terms of instrumental music. Giacomo Setaccioli (1968-25), an accomplished writer of both chamber music and opera, probably drew closer to his European contemporaries than any other of his compatriots. Unfortunately, the vast majority of his output was lost during the first part of the new century and his contribution to Italian romanticism can only be reconstructed through the few pieces that have remained. Of these his *Sonata* for clarinet and piano (op.31, date unknown) merits special attention, since its masterful writing rivals that of similar works by Brahms. The texture, however, is often lighter than what one would normally expect from the German romantics and a surprising foretaste of Ravel can be heard in some of the more brilliant piano excursions or in the gently lilting harmonies of the piece's central movement.

Finally, one more important name should be added to our list. As an accomplished organist of international repute it is no surprise that Marco Enrico Bossi (1861-1925) dedicated much of his time to the long overdue task of renewing and reviving the Italian repertoire for his instrument. At the end of the 19th century organ recitals more often than not consisted of arrangements of well-known operatic pieces, a custom that did little to advance compositional or performing technique and almost totally neglected the once glorious tradition of Italian organ music dating back to the baroque period and beyond.

Like many other progressively minded composers Bossi followed the wise words of Verdi and 'looked back to move forward'. A thorough review of Bach together with a serious appraisal of the technical and linguistic advances that had in the meantime taken place outside of Italy, notably in the hands of César Franck, enabled him to restore some dignity to Italian organ music. In addition to his numerous pieces for organ Bossi also wrote vocal and instrumental music, including works combining organ and orchestra such as the *Concerto in A minor* (op.100, 1900), where we can hear an opulent and overtly Italian melodic vein kept in order by a moderate dose of 'nordic' discipline.

As we have already suggested, the achievements of this small group of Italians are all the more remarkable considering the musical environment in which they had evolved. It is hard for us to imagine that until the 1860s the symphonic music of Mendelsohn, Schumann and even Beethoven was still virtually unknown in Italy. And towards the end of the century audiences had to be carefully weaned onto the music of Brahms and Liszt before they were anywhere near being ready for the likes of Mahler or Richard Strauss, not to mention Debussy. The antagonism that *Pelléas et Mélisande* met with in 1907 has already been mentioned, but as late as 1911 Strauss's *Der Rosenkavalier* was still considered too modern for the ears of the audience at La Scala.

The inevitable result of such isolation from the European mainstream was that, notwithstanding all good intentions, the pioneers of 'new Italian music' were never likely to produce anything really innovative. Their output in reality barely scratches the surface of what the well-established giants were producing outside of Italy.[1] The only

---

1/ Fortunately they were able to pass their 'mission' on to the next generation: Martucci was to teach Respighi, while Bossi counted among his pupils both Ghedini (who later taught Berio) and Malipiero (who in turn taught Maderna).

option left open to many forward-looking composers was therefore to turn their back on the problem and go abroad. This often meant travelling just a short distance across the Alps, but in musical terms it was like embarking on a voyage to the other side of the world.

Leone Sinigaglia (1868-1944) undertook such a journey in 1893 when he went to study in Vienna and later in Prague. In these important musical centres he not only made friends with Brahms and Mahler, but also came into contact with Dvorak, probably his most important model. From the latter he learnt to appreciate the value of national folksong and on his return to Turin he set to work on the collection of traditional songs and melodies of the Piedmont region.

Although his music could be said to be somewhat lacking in depth, Sinigaglia's attempts to incorporate popular music into so-called cultured music established him as one of the first Italians to be caught up in a fashion which was to prove so important in the development of early 20th century music. And yet the Italian public were not at all convinced of the suitability of such 'vulgar' elements for the 'refined' atmosphere of the concert-hall. At a concert given in Turin in 1905 where the programme included his *Danze Piemontesi* (op. 31) the audience were quick to show their disapproval. He nevertheless remained unperturbed and continued to collect and draw inspiration from folk songs. His orchestral suite *Piemonte* (op. 36, 1909) epitomises his style, showing a strong influence of Dvorak not only in certain harmonic progressions, but above all in the treatment of the lighter dance-like passages where the folk tunes are given new life.

A similar fate befell Ferruccio Busoni (1866-1924), who at first chose and was later virtually forced to spend most of his life abroad. A combination of mixed parentage (his mother was of German origin) and strong character led him to achieve results that were far more enduring and certainly more uncompromising than those of other Italian composers of his generation. What most distinguishes him from his contemporaries is the astonishing development in style and idiom that took place during his relatively short life. The initial influence of Brahms in the youthful piano pieces soon gave way to a freer approach to structure which owed much to the rhapsodic writing of Liszt. But it was his lifelong passion for Bach and his consequent adoption of devices such as the fugue, chaconne and passacaglia that really led him away from the late romantic tendencies which were slowly creeping into the contemporary Italian scene. What eventually emerges is an original and very personal form of neo-classicism mixed with more than a hint of expressionism.

The suffocating musical environment prevalent in Italy in the early 1900s was clearly no place for such a forward-looking figure to mature. For almost twenty years he travelled extensively, covering much of Europe and spending three years in the USA where he taught, conducted and performed. Finally, in 1894 he settled in Berlin, at that time a thriving artistic city and above all an important centre for cultural innovation. Yet despite his choice to reside abroad Busoni appears to have nourished a dream to return to his homeland and head a movement for the renewal of Italian music. His short-lived attempt to re-establish himself in Italy by taking up the post of Director of the Bologna Conservatory was soon thwarted by the outbreak of the First World War, which practically forced him once again into exile on account of his foreign connections. By the time the air had cleared his ill-health prevented him from fulfilling his dream.

Due to his long absences from Italy Busoni is often overlooked as a key figure in the history of his country's music. In reality he was following a parallel path to that of other would-be reformers. In his opera *Arlecchino* (1915), for example, he looks back to the *Commedia dell'Arte* for inspiration in the same way that Wolf-Ferrari had done. And his now overshadowed version of *Turandot* (1917) was based on the same play by the 18th century Venetian writer Gozzi that was to shortly to inspire Puccini. Busoni's version of *Turandot* offers a much more formal representation of the story and certainly retains more of the original classical spirit. His attitude towards *opera lirica* was, in fact, one of open distain and when he conceived his last opera *Doktor Faustus* (1916-1924) he sincerely believed that he was writing a work that would finally clear away the vestiges of *verismo* and that would be used as a model by future generations. As it turned out he died before the work could be completed. And the political circumstances at the time were not, in any case, particularly favourable for the fulfilment of his aspirations.

Like Sinigaglia, Busoni was fascinated by the simplicity of folk music, and they also provided him with the chance to experiment with modes which were not strictly major or minor. His main source of inspiration, however, came from a little further afield. During his travels in the USA he came into contact with the songs and chants of the Native Indians and became determined to incorporate them in some way into his own music. His *Indianische Fantasia* for piano and orchestra (op.44, 1913) is based on a number of such melodies, although they are often shrouded in a swirl of Lisztian cadences. On the other hand, his smaller scale *Indian Diary Book One* for piano (1915) tries a simpler setting, in some ways reminiscent of the approach adopted by Bartok and Kodaly.

Busoni is now remembered most of all for his masterly transcriptions of J.S.Bach, where the fugues and passacaglias are made to shine in a strange new light. But musicologists tend to be more interested in his highly original and little known theoretical writings. In his 'Sketch for a New Aesthetic of Music' (1906) not only did he predict the use of scales based on all 12 notes of the octave, but he also proposed the division of tones and semitones into smaller parts (third-tones and sixth-tones), an idea that was to be taken seriously and put into practice only many years later. Just how revolutionary these notions actually were can be understood from the fact that in the Italian translation of the book (originally written in German) all references to such micro-divisions were mysteriously omitted. The average Italian musician of the time would probably have found such a concept quite perplexing.

Although society, and technology, was not quite ready for his advanced theories, in some of his more mature works Busoni practically abandoned tonality. It is, for example, stretched to its utmost limits in the *Berceuse Elégiaque* op.42 (1910), a work that places the composer in line with the earlier experiments of the new Viennese school. And it is no mere chance that Schoenberg himself took a special interest in this piece and actually transcribed the work for a chamber group (c.1920). A further step in the same direction can be seen in the Second *Sonatina* for piano (1912) where the composer's wish to free himself from the conventions of the previous century are apparent not only in the virtual atonality of much of the piece, but also in his decision at a certain point to dispense with bar lines[1].

While Busoni was proposing such seemingly outrageous ideas in his 'Sketch', another much more drastic revolution was being proposed by the so-called Futurists. As well as embracing both visual art and music the movement also covered more mundane areas of everyday life including fashion and even cooking. The founder of the movement, Filippo Tommaso Marinetti (1876-1944), was himself a poet, but called the world of art in general to arms in his notorious 'manifesto' which was first published in the French newspaper *Le Figaro* in 1909. Basically he proposed a total revolt against the academicism and institutionalism of the past which was to be replaced by a language truly representative of the needs and realities of the modern world . Other 'manifestos' followed and in 1910 it was the turn of Francesco Balilla Pratella (1880-1955) to write his first Manifesto of Futurism in music.[2]

Pratella was apparently not a particularly gifted composer. He even failed to gain a place at the Bologna Conservatory, a fact that may in some way have encouraged him to take up a cause which, among other things, advocated the closure of all conventional musical conservatories. His musical output includes many small-scale piano pieces and various theatrical works including his most well known composition, the opera *L'aviatore Drò* (1915-20). Musically speaking the opera shows a certain influence of the impressionists, but from a historical point of view it is notable above all for its total avoidance of melodic arias, quite a courageous step for an Italian composer brought up in a provincial musical environment where melody was paramount to success. Despite the enthusiasm of Marinetti, who was

---

1/The American composer Charles Ives immediately comes to mind. It is probably no coincidence that Busoni had previously spent some time in New England.

2/ For the political implications of the Futurist manifestos, see Chapter 4.

present at the first performance in 1920 and hailed the work as a 'triumph' for the Futurist movement, the success of Drò was somewhat short-lived. The work has been occasionally been revived, but more for its curiosity value than for its artistic worth.

Ironically, despite all his grand designs to revolutionise the whole Italian musical scene, Pratella's most noble achievement was probably his collection of traditional folk songs from his native Romagna. To be fair this was in every way coherent with his futurist philosophy which saw folk music as the deepest expression of genuine music, uncontaminated as it was by the horrors of the academics. And of course his interest in popular music does draw him closer to other composers of the time who were involved in similar projects.

If, however, we wish to search for the real innovator within the movement we should look beyond Pratella to his friend and fellow futurist Luigi Russolo (1885-1947). Although he originally joined the

Pratella (right) with the poet Marinetti (left)

Pratella (left) and Mascagni (second left)

movement as an artist, his biggest contribution was undoubtedly that of being one of the first composers in the western world to introduce pure noise into music. In 1913 he contributed to the series of Futurist manifestos with his *L'Arte dei Rumori* (the Art of Noises) which supported the movement's philosophy of releasing music from the constraints of tradition and advocated free improvisation based on the sounds and noises of the modern industrialised world.

In order to accomplish his highly revolutionary aims Russolo invented a series of purpose-built machines collectively defined as 'intonarumori' (noisemakers). Needless to say in a society that found it hard to accept the music of Debussy the reaction of the Milan audience to a concert in 1914 presenting 18 'intonarumori' leaves little to the imagination. And a similar fate lay in store for his series of concerts at the London Coliseum later in the same year.

After presenting his futuristic instruments in concerts which took him to various European capitals, Russolo finally reached Paris in 1921 where he found a much more suitable climate for his experiments. It was here that he came into contact with other important innovators like Ravel and Stravinsky, who took a great interest in his work and encouraged him to persevere. He later patented a keyboard instrument called the 'rumoramonio'(noiseharmonium) which was capable of producing quarter tones and even smaller intervals. This invention was destined to capture the imagination of Varèse, who in 1929 organised a concert involving several of Russolo's instruments.

Unfortunately the fantastic machines were fated to end their lives in Paris where they were abandoned and eventually destroyed during the Second World War. There are many written accounts of his exhibitions and the reactions of the various audiences around Europe, but sadly only a single poor-quality recording has survived to bear witness to the work of Europe's first advocate of 'musique concrète'.

The proposals and ideals of the Futurists were, without doubt, far ahead of their time. If we consider that it was not until the last few decades of the 20th century that the use of manipulated or elaborated 'noise' became commonplace, the astonishing insight of the group appears all the more remarkable. In the end one is left with the suspicion that the ultimate reason for their downfall was simply a lack of any real musical talent. And this notion is supported by the fact that Pratella, supposedly the most important composer of the group, was refused admission to the *Società nazionale italiana di Musica Moderna* founded by Casella in 1917.

We shall leave the last words to the critic of a British newspaper who wrote the following comment in a review of Russolo's London concerts: "The sounds of a great city, such as signor Russolo has attempted to portray, are intensely polyrhythmic, but he has reduced them to the strictest of common time. It results that his compositions are (...) curiously old-fashioned in construction. The instruments may be 'futurist', but what they perform harks back to Donizetti. In rhythmic resource his 'futurist' art is many generations behind the music of Stravinsky."[1]

1/ *Futurist Music Fiasco* (Pall Mall Gazette, 16th June 1914).

3

THE DAWN OF A NEW ERA

Some revolutions, as history has taught us, can be very short-lived. And so it was that the sweeping reforms proposed on the one hand by Busoni and on the other by Pratella and his fellow Futurists came to little or nothing. Real change was to be a slow and methodical process and was largely the result of the dedicated work of a series of composers born in and around the 1880s.

The challenge that this generation faced, now that Sgambati and other pioneers had cleared the way, was to produce a new strain of genuinely Italian music that took into account modern tendencies from abroad without merely ending up as poor copies of certain influential non-Italian composers. Several Italians did, in fact, succumb to this fate and have, for one reason or another, been long forgotten. It is sufficient to glance through the titles of the would-be impressionist composer Francesco Santoliquido (1883-1971) to realise that he had rather overstepped the mark. They include: *Crepuscolo sul mare* (twilight at sea), *Chiarità lunare* (moonlight) and *Giardini notturni* (nocturnal gardens).[1]

Composers such as Vincenzo Tommasini (1978-1950) more successfully bridged the gap between Italy and the rest of Europe by setting to music works of 19th century Italian poets (in particular

---

1/ Santoliquido is nevertheless saved from total oblivion by his genuine attempts to incorporate elements of Arabic music into many of his works.

poems by Carducci and Leopardi) using a style that incorporates elements of both the French mélodie and the late romantic German Lied, while retaining more than an echo of the late 19th century Italian romanzo. Moreover, Tommasini's contribution to the reappraisal of the Italian Baroque was by no means small and he was among the first to rediscover and subsequently popularise the music of composers like Domenico Scarlatti. His ballet *Le donne di buon umore* (1917), based on pieces by Scarlatti, could be singled out as a landmark in the development of Italian neo-classicism and predates by two years Stravinsky's more famous *Pulcinella* (a similar idea using the music of Pergolesi).[1]

Verdi would doubtlessly have gained no small satisfaction from such developments, as his advice to young composers to respect the glorious Italian past was at last bearing fruit. We have already seen, for instance, how leading composers of the new generation such as Wolf-Ferrari had begun to draw inspiration from the classical comedies of Goldoni. Their efforts were not necessarily confined to their own compositions, since many were also actively involved in the actual physical revival of the works of forgotten composers. In 1907, for example, Wolf-Ferrari helped to organise a performance of the Goldonian opera *Il filosofo di Campagna* by the 18th century Venetian composer Galuppi.

The arduous task of revisiting forgotten works was not, of course, left entirely to the composers. The first decades of the 20th century saw a rapid rise in the importance of the musicologist and already at the end of the 19th century the foundations for the rediscovery of so-called ancient music had been laid by long forgotten enthusiasts like Oscar Chilesotti (1848-1916) and Luigi Torchi (1858-1920). Another important figure, Giovanni Tebaldini (1864-1952), dedicated much of his life to the study and revival of Gregorian chant and Renaissance polyphony and was able to transmit his enthusiasm to his numerous pupils.

But when speaking of musicologists of the early 20th century the

---

1/ Tommasini also collaborated with Smareglia in the completion of Boito's opera *Nerone* (first performed 1924).

name that inevitably springs to mind is that of Fausto Torrefranca (1883-1955), a writer and critic famous above all for the bitter attack on Italian melodrama in his article '*Puccini e l'opera internationale*' (1930). His true importance, though, lies in the leading role he played in the rediscovery of the Italian Baroque and Renaissance. He was one of the first writers to insist on and subsequently demonstrate the central role played by early Italian music in the development of the classical sonata and the symphony, something that we nowadays take for granted. In addition, he was particularly active in the campaign to establish the History of Music as a subject to be taught in music schools and conservatories and from 1913 onwards he was to become professor of this very subject at various Italian universities.

During this period of heated debate the role of the music critic also came into its own. Of particular interest is the contribution of Giannotto Bastianelli (1883-1927), who was instrumental in gathering forces against what he saw as the decadent state into which Italian music had fallen. In 1911 he published a manifesto largely inspired by the 'heroic' work of the Russian nationalist group 'The Five', where he proposed the formation of a group of like-minded Italian musicians. Together with Bastianelli the Italian 'Cinque' were to include R.Bossi, Pizzetti, Malipiero and Respighi. In the end, though, the group never really materialised and each of them followed their own interests which eventually took them in quite different directions. Incidentally, of the four composers in question only Rinaldo Renzo Bossi (1883-1965), the son of M.E.Bossi, failed to make his mark and is now remembered mostly for his teaching activity, initially in Milan and later in Venice.

In the meantime aid for the cause was to come from unsuspected quarters. A fascinating character whose name regularly appears throughout the careers of many European musicians active during the first decades of the century was that of Elizabeth Sprague Coolidge (1864-1963), an American millionairess who dedicated much of her life to commissioning works, above all chamber music, and sponsoring concerts to promote modern music. During her frequent visits to Europe she often travelled to Italy and involved many of the most important contemporary musicians in her projects and social gatherings. And she took great joy in organising meetings between the Italians and such distinguished names as Stravinsky and Schoenberg.

One of the fortunate Italians to benefit from such gatherings was Ottorino Respighi (1879-1936), a composer whose music represents an interesting case of the fusion between old and new. At first glance Respighi's interest in early music would appear to have been quite slow in manifesting itself, especially as far as his larger-scale works are concerned. Apart from the occasional references to plainsong woven into the fabric of the well-known Roman trilogy (*Fontane di Roma*, 1916; *Pini di Roma*, 1924; *Feste Romane*, 1928) his most familiar contribution to the revival of early music is in the suite *Gli Uccelli* (1927), a suite featuring arrangements of pieces by various baroque composers. Less frequently performed are the three delicately orchestrated suites of *Antiche Arie e Danze per Liuto* (1917, 1923, 1931) that were written almost side by side with the much more sumptuous symphonic poems. The titles of two other mature works written by Respighi in the 1920s leave little doubt as to their source of inspiration: both the *Concerto Gregoriano* (1921) and the *Concerto in Modo Misolodio* (1924) are clearly based on ancient non-diatonic modes.

In reality Respighi's interest in the field of ancient music dates back almost to the beginning of his career. His orchestral transcription of Monteverdi's *Il Lamento di Arianna*, for example, obtained considerable success in Berlin as early as 1908, the same year that saw his re-elaboration of the 'lost' violin sonatas of Vivaldi, Tartini and other baroque masters who are now familiar household names, but at the time were still quite obscure. Echoes of the past can also be heard in an early group of songs entitled 5 *Canti all'antica* (1906). While not making any direct reference to pre-romantic idioms, these simple settings of verses based on the 14th century writer Boccaccio display a sobriety and restraint not at all common in Italian vocal music of the period.

It may perhaps seem a little surprising to speak of restraint in a composer notorious for his orchestral fireworks. Allegedly, Respighi's skill in handling the orchestra derives mainly from his trip to Russia and subsequent meeting with Rimsky-Korsakov, a recognised master of instrumentation, and he may well have spoken with the Russian master on various occasions. But there appears to be no real documentary evidence that the young Italian actually studied under the Rimsky-Korsakov. Nevertheless, his admiration and the consequent influence are real enough and the impressive command of orchestration displayed in Respighi's larger works often results in an orgy of colour which at times borders on the excessive. Yet many of Respighi's lesser known works, ranging from the ethereal song-cycle *Il tramonto* (1918) to the lightly-scored *Trittico Botticelliano* for chamber orchestra (1927), are marked by a calm reserve that bears witness to the existence of a much gentler side to the composer's nature.

Towards the end of his life Respighi appears to have become increasingly obsessed with writing opera, almost as if he wished, in the end, to be part of an aspect of Italian music that many of his generation were, on the contrary, trying leave behind them. After writing a handful of operatic works at the beginning of his career which met with limited success – one in particular, *Marie-Victoire* (1907-09) had to wait until 2004 for its first performance – his enthusiasm for the genre seems to have suddenly returned some twenty years later, at a time when Mussolini was doing his best to save Italy's fading operatic tradition. His three major operas (*La Campane Sommersa*, 1927; *Maria Egiziaca*, 1932; *La Fiamma*, 1934) all met with a clamorous, albeit short-lived success in Italy, while descriptions of their reception in countries with a large migrant Italian population, in particular Argentina and the USA, cannot help but remind us of the hero's welcome given to Mascagni at the start of the century.[1]

The desire to write opera does not, of course, preclude innovation. Another composer born in the same period, Ildebrando Pizzetti (1880-1968), wrote a total of 14 operas, but far from wishing to continue in the well-established line of the melodrama, his intention was quite the opposite. His ambition was to breathe new life into Italian

---

1/ Significantly, Toscanini excused himself from conducting the New York première of *Maria Egiziaca* in 1932 and the same work met with a cold reception at its Paris première in 1934 For the respective attitudes of Respighi and Toscanini towards fascism see Chapter 4.

opera by introducing a very free declamatory style which incorporated much of what he had learned from his teacher Tebaldini about the flexibility of rhythm and melody characteristic of Renaissance music. Pizzetti's fascination with vocal music and above all with the theatre is apparent right from his first important work, the incidental music for Gabriele D'Annunzio's play *La nave* (1908).

A long association between the two artists ensued, even though Pizzetti openly declared that he preferred to write his own librettos. In the words of one critic, to work with a text by D'Annunzio was tantamount to placing the composer in a 'straight-jacket'.[1] Both the words and music of his second opera *Débora e Jaèle* (1922) were in fact written by the composer himself, although the idea again came from D'Annuzio. The result was a work that could be said to represent a turning point in the history of Italian opera. Not only did it offer an alternative to the *verismo* vogue, but it also made few concessions to the chromaticism of Wagner or the impressionism of Debussy. A truly Italian opera, then, remarkable in particular for its near-perfect conciliation between the natural rhythm of the words and their setting to music. This aspect continued to be fundamental throughout the whole of Pizzetti's career, reaching its peak in one of his last operas, *L'assassinio nella Cattedrale* (1958). Here, as in the majority of his theatrical works, it is interesting to note how the orchestra tends to be given a supporting role (though not one of mere accompaniment) and, apart from the haunting cor anglais solo at the opening of the intermezzo, is entrusted with remarkably few melodies.

Still in the realm of vocal music, Pizzetti's contribution to the smaller scale Italian song or *Lirica* is quite significant, given that there had never been any real *Lieder* tradition in Italy or, apart from the early songs of Respighi, anything to match the then flourishing French *chanson* or *mélodie*. Although he regularly returned to the genre sporadically throughout the whole of his career, one of the best examples can be heard in an early song, *I pastori* (1908), a setting of a poem by D'Annunzio, where an unmistakably lyrical vein is combined with an

---

1/ Carlo Parmentola in his entry on Pizzetti in the *Dizionario della Musica e dei Musicisti* (UTET, Torino 1994).

unusually meticulous attention to the natural rhythm of the words.

The influence of song is also distinguishable in the vast majority of Pizzetti's instrumental pieces, not only in those with specific references to vocal forms such as the *Tre Canti* for violin/cello and piano (1924), but also in the lyrical themes of, for example, the *Sonata* for violin and piano (1919) and the *Piano trio* in A major (1925). A hint of organum can be heard at the opening of the second movement of the *Trio*, testifying to the inevitable influence of Debussy, but more especially to the composer's indebtedness to ancient vocal music. And despite the fact that he wrote a fair number of works for larger forces, including concertos for piano, cello and violin (1930, 1934 and 1945 respectively), as well as a symphony (1940), references to the voice and theatre are never far away. The piano concerto bears the title *Canti della stagione alta* ('songs of the high season'), while other pieces, including an intermezzo and numerous overtures, derive directly from theatrical usage.

After his death performances of his works, especially those written for the theatre, gradually declined until virtually disappearing from the repertory. This could be partially explained by the fact that Pizzetti's musical creativity never really reached the high (or low) points which characterise the work of certain of his contemporaries whose work has been less neglected.

As with many other Italians of the time, his search for a modern idiom manifested itself more in his theoretical writings than in his music. But even here he was not willing to venture too far across the line. Significantly, the collaboration between the composer and Bastianelli on such projects as the journal 'Dissonanza', which had been founded in 1914 expressly to promote modern music in Italy, eventually broke down due to what the critic saw as Pizzetti's innate conservatism (ironically Pizzetti's music was never exceptionally 'dissonant').

There were of course many other successful composers who were fundamentally much more 'conservative' than Pizzetti. Among these we find two names, Victor De Sabata (1892-1967) and Vittorio Gui (1885-1975), who were important mostly for their work as conduc-

tors and promoters of modern music, but, like many conductors, also
tried their hand at composition. Given the period in question it was
inevitable that they were heavily influenced by their contact with the
music of Wagner and Richard Strauss, two composers who may have
appeared modern at the time, but were soon to be superseded. Nevertheless they were both held in extremely high esteem very early
in their careers and the critic G.M.Gatti went so far as to describe
De Sabata as "one of the most gifted of contemporary Italian composers"[1]. Interestingly, one or two pieces from De Sabata's small but
popular output have actually managed to stand the test of time and
his symphonic poem *Juventus* (1919) still puts in an occasional ap-
pearance in concert programmes. Time has been less generous in the
case of Gui, whose modest list of works (including two operas and
various orchestral and choral pieces) would seem to have completely
disappeared from the scene.

We now come to the two composers who undoubtedly represent
the mainstay of Italian music in the first half of the 20th century.
Francesco Malipiero (1882-1973) and Alfredo Casella (1883-1947)
were both involved in the redefinition of their national musical language. But unlike many of their contemporaries they really practised
what they preached and eagerly explored paths that would take them
much closer to their European counterparts.

It is difficult to talk about Malipiero without using the word 'prolific'. His output, spanning almost seventy years, was nothing less
than enormous and included numerous operas, eleven symphonies,
eight string quartets, various concertos, as well as a vast quantity of
other vocal, orchestral and chamber works. He was one of the first of
what turned out to be a new wave of important Venetian composers
who were destined to restore the city's musical pride to its former
noble levels.[2] During his formative years visits to important European capitals such as Vienna and Berlin had naturally led to a strong
late Romantic strain in his earliest compositions, and the guidance

---

1/ *The Musical Times* (April 1921)

2/ His numerous pupils included Maderna and Nono, both of paramount importance to the musical fame of Venice.

Malipiero (left) with Maderna (right)

of his Italian teacher M.E.Bossi had probably done little to modify this stance. But in 1913 he took the drastic step of destroying most of what he had written in his youth with a mind to exploring fresh horizons. The few remaining examples of his early work, notably the *Canto Notturno* for baritone and orchestra (1910), display a distinctly Central European bent.

Subsequently, after shaking off the inevitable influence of the French impressionists whose music he had encountered at first hand during his visits to France and in particular to Paris, it was once again the study of 16th and 17th century music that had the deepest influence on Malipiero's mature style. This resulted in a 'softening' of the traditional diatonic system through the use of ancient modes and the 'release' of the melody from any formal constraints by adopting something similar to the free-moving lines typical of Gregorian chant and monody. He also made a vast number of transcriptions of early Italian music and was actively involved in arranging complete editions of the works of composers such as Monteverdi and Vivaldi who had contributed so much to the fame of his native city. It is no mere chance that the first of his eleven symphonies (1933) is sub-titled 'in *quattro tempi come le quattro stagioni*' ('in four movements like the four seasons').

In his determination to develop a musical language of his own Malipiero took up a radical stand against the excesses of late romanticism and soon began to abandon any notion of formal thematic development in favour of a continuous evolution of melodic lines. This is well illustrated in the series of symphonic impressions entitled *Pause del silenzio* (1917), where themes appear and disappear without undergoing any development in the traditional sense. Furthermore, the juxtaposition of clearly contrasting sections characterising this work, with moments of intense emotion set against moments of calm or simple joy, was eventually to become a hallmark of his later compositions. This feature can be clearly heard throughout his eleven symphonies, which were not traditional works like those of Martucci, who had deliberately tried to emulate the great symphonic forms of 19th century, but were fundamentally episodic in structure and in the place of themes we often find meandering strands of melody coloured by the use of non-diatonic modes.

A natural extension of his 'anti-romantic' sentiment was expressed in his early rejection of Italian verismo opera, which he once described as nothing but a brief digression in the history of a country with a glorious musical past. His first significant theatrical work, *Sette canzoni* (1919), could in fact be said to defy any form of historical definition. It is almost totally devoid of dramatic action, or even a storyline, and consists of seven different scenes featuring the musical representation of seven mediaeval poems, which are loosely linked by recurring themes but contain no real dramatic development as such.

Malipiero was at first accused of being influenced by German expressionism, a movement that was not seen at all favourably in the nationalistic climate predominant in the Italy of the post-war years. Regardless of such criticism he continued to apply this technique to a greater or lesser extent in all the theatrical pieces he conceived over the following decade, culminating in what is generally considered to be his masterpiece of the genre, the *Torneo Notturno* (1929). Once again seven songs, or nocturnes in this case, are presented side by side with a minimum of common thematic material, no recitative and no dramatic development. This particular technique of using starkly contrasting and often unrelated blocks of material to construct his 'operas' was soon to become known as '*teatro a pannelli*' (literally, 'theatre in panels'), a term that became synonymous with the name of Malipiero.

His experimental approach to theatre was nevertheless rudely interrupted in 1934 with the unfortunate episode surrounding *La favola del figlio cambiato* (the apparent censorship levelled against this work will be dealt with in more detail in Chapter 4). From a musical point of view the piece appears remarkably adventurous on account of the use of widely contrasting musical styles, including a return to the use of recitative, some elements of jazz, hints at atonality and even references to children's nursery rhymes. From a structural point of view, though, the opera could be said to be more traditional than many of his previous works, since it presents a regular story-line giving the work an overall dramatic unity that the composer seemed to have deliberately avoided in his other operas.

The few theatrical works that Malipiero produced in the years immediately following this ill-fated work display a marked return to traditional lyric opera. Similarly, many of the orchestral works written in this period, for example the *Concerto per violoncello ed orchestra* (1937), seem to have lost their innovative bite. Whether this is a mere coincidence or the direct result of some kind of censorship is still an open question. The fact remains that it was not until 1942, when the fascist régime was nearing its end, that the composer returned to writing his characteristic *teatro a pannelli*, a path that he was never to completely abandon again despite any subsequent development in other aspects of his musical language. His *Capricci di Callot* written in that very year not only returns to the former style but also has a marked neo-classical taste in its combination of vocal music and dance, where the characters are dressed up in allegorical masks and costumes, very much in the style of a 16th century 'entertainment'.

The mid-fifties marked a turning point in Malipiero's career. He was truly fascinated by the experiments in atonality that had been taking place over the previous thirty years, but like many other Italian composers of his generation he had chosen to admire such revolutionary figures as Schoenberg from a safe distance.[1] Nevertheless his *Fantasie Concertanti* (1954) display a noticeable move towards a more chromatic idiom, which becomes even more pronounced in the 8 *Dialoghi* (1956-57), a fascinating series of introspective compositions which range from pieces for chamber orchestra to intimate small-scale concertos.

But despite the extreme chromaticism found in later works such as the 10th Symphony (1967) the barrier of tonality was never truly breached. Even though he outlived most of his contemporaries and during his long life had witnessed countless changes and movements, he remained faithful to his original source of inspiration, the music of the Renaissance and the Baroque. In 1952 he had paid tribute to Vivaldi in a collection called *Vivaldiana* and it is no mere chance that one of his very last works, *Gabrieliana* (1971), was a tribute to another great Venetian master.

Although originally setting out with similar aims, Malipiero and his fellow innovator Casella were eventually to take quite divergent paths. Malipiero's obvious reference to Stravinsky's *Petroushka* in the opening of his *La bottega da Caffè*, the first of his *Tre Commedie Goldoniane* (1926), would seem to indicate that both composers were breathing

---

1/ He paid homage to Schoenberg in his one of his very last orchestral works *Omaggio a Belmonte* (1971)

the same air at least for the first half of their careers. There is, on the other hand, little doubt that Malipiero's major source of inspiration was vocal music, while Casella was from the beginning a composer of music that was essentially instrumental in concept. The few songs that he wrote, in many cases just a poor imitation of the French chanson, were on the whole quite insignificant. Even his most well known vocal work, the opera *La Donna Serpente* (op.50, 1932), took him three years to complete and had initially been conceived as a ballet.

Like many composers and artists of his generation Casella spent much of his early career in Paris. But apart from youthful pieces such as the *Pavane* (op.1, 1901-02) for piano, Casella has surprisingly little to show for his close associations with the likes of Fauré and Ravel. By the time he composed the *Pagine di Guerra* (op.25, 1915), a collection of short pieces for piano duet written after almost 20 years of living in France, his idiom had become aggressive and almost Bartokian in its use of dissonant harmony and percussive rhythm. It should, of course, be remembered that Paris was also the home, if not the birthplace, of Stravinsky's neo-classicism and a fair measure of contagion, or perhaps even adulation, was inevitable. The influence of Stravinsky was destined to continue throughout his life: it is still quite apparent in what is probably the composer's most popular and certainly most recorded work, the *Serenata* for chamber ensemble (op.46, 1927-30), while echoes can still be heard in the much later *Divertimento per Fulvia* (op.64, 1940).

On his return to Italy Casella was determined to make good use of all the novelties he had absorbed during his long absence. In 1917 he founded the *Società Italiana di Musica Moderna*, whose principal aim, as the name suggests, was to encourage the modernisation of music in his own country. This did not mean that he indiscriminately accepted all that was hailed as modern. His refusal to accept Pratella into the society has already been mentioned and in general he had little admiration for the Futurists, a movement that was slowly but surely losing its way amidst the political turmoil of the time. He nevertheless granted permission for his *Puppazzetti* (op.27, 1915) to be used in the *Balli Plastici*, a futuristic ballet which was put together in 1918 for a puppet theatre in Rome and which also featured music by Malipiero and the British composer Lord Berners. In the grotesque twists and turns of the five dance-like pieces that make up the *Puppazzetti*, originally written for piano duet and later transcribed for small instrumental ensemble, it is impossible not to notice the mark of Erik Satie, a sort of spiritual leader for the 'alternative' movement active in Paris at the time of Casella's residence.

Dance forms, whether deriving from the classical suite or from popular folklore, were actually the staple diet of Casella's music and movements entitled minuet, gavotte, gigue and tarantella commonly appear in both early and mature works. And yet the influence of popular music as such tends to be limited to these pseudo-dances, for he was never truly caught up in the fashionable research into folk music. His reference to the folklore of Sicily in his adaptation of Pirandello's *La Giara* for a ballet (op.41, 1924) may perhaps have been the first symptoms of an enforced nationalism rather than the fulfilment of any artistic or spiritual necessity. We shall leave such matters to the next chapter where we shall also discuss the somewhat atypical works, including several concertos and a symphony, written by the composer during the 1930s after suffering ruthless attacks from patriotic and anti-modernist factions.

Casella's involvement in the reappraisal of what he called 'il grande passato nostro strumentale' ('our great instrumental past') was genuine enough. He made several transcriptions of works by Baroque and Classical composers and, following in the steps of Tommasini in his tribute to Scarlatti, Casella wrote *Scarlattiana* (op.44, 1926) for piano and chamber orchestra. And like Malipiero his tribute to Italy's musical patrimony culminated in one of his last compositions, a divertimento called *Paganiniana* (op.65, 1942).

Finally, it would be a pity to conclude this chapter dedicated to Italian composers born in the last two decades of the 19th century without mentioning a rather unusual case. We have already seen how the fusion of art and music was becoming increasingly important at the turn of the new century. The futurist exponent Russolo, for example, had begun his creative life as a visual artist and only subsequently did he decide to divert his energies into music.

The name Savinio probably means little to even the most ardent scholars of twentieth century music, but if his real name, Andrea De Chirico, were to be used a few eyebrows would doubtlessly be raised. Alberto Savinio (1891-1952) was in reality the pseudonym chosen by the brother of Giorgio De Chirico, the celebrated surrealist painter. In addition to his work as an artist and critic, Savinio dedicated two short periods of his life to composing music. The first (and probably the most interesting) coincided with his move to Paris in 1910. Here he came into contact with the leading representatives of the avant-garde in all sectors of art and culture. Like Casella he was not particularly influenced by the flourishing impressionist movement, but rather by the alternative route offered by the likes of Erik Satie. While his philosophy coincided in many ways with that of the Futurists, he disliked this label and preferred to call himself a 'Sincerist', implying that he was willing to accept 'all that was available to be heard' whether it belonged to the past, present or future. For this reason it is not uncommon to find passages in his work where the very latest compositional techniques are employed within an idiom reminiscent of 19th century romanticism (clear echoes of Robert Schumann can often be heard).

During his stay in Paris Savinio had the privilege of attending the first performances of Stravinsky's *Petroushka* and the *Rite of Spring*, both of which made an enormous impression on him. He later collaborated with Stravinsky not as a musician, but as a designer for a production of *Oedipus Rex* in Milan. The music he wrote in these early Paris years displays an almost obsessive use of polytonality or bitonality and almost any page opened at random from works like the piano suite *Les chants de la mi-mort* (1913-15) or the *Chants étranges* (1914-15) will supply examples. Such features still appear in the handful of works he wrote during his later musical period (1948-51), but out of their original historical context they no longer have the impact of his earlier works. His ballet *Vita dell'uomo* (1948) and the one-act opera *Orfeo vedovo* (1950) show, if anything, a softening of tone and, more significantly, a total refusal of the innovations that surrounded him in the years following the Second World War.

4

A FASCIST INTERLUDE

At the end of October 1922 the leaders of the fast-growing Italian fascist movement organised the notorious 'March on Rome', an event that was destined to change the course of European history. King Vittorio Emanuele III ignored all pleas from his government to send in the troops and immediately gave in to the demands of the fascists. A few days later, at the beginning of November, Puccini wrote to Mussolini congratulating him on his enterprise and offering him his best wishes for the new government.

This is not to suggest, of course, that Puccini was necessarily an ardent supporter of fascism as we know it today. But it does confirm that, as is often the case when dealing with historical events, the situation needs to be viewed in a much broader context. In the year in question the new political movement was still in its early days (there can be no talk of a dictatorship before 1925, by which time Puccini was already dead) and few people were really sure what it really stood for or what would eventually come out of it. But like many other middle-class Italians, Puccini was no doubt attracted to the idea of a return to traditional values coupled with a revival of his country's past glories. Interestingly, between the years 1935 and 1943, when Mussolini was at the height of his power, there were no fewer than 87 performances of Puccini's operas during the various seasons in Italian theatres and festivals, a record second only to that of Verdi.[1]

The history of fascism is by no means straightforward. It would be

---

1 For these and other fascinating statistics see F. Nicolodi's book *Musica e Musicisti nel Ventennio Fascita* (Discanto, Fiesole 1984).

a serious misinterpretation of history to imagine that the unbending ideals and policies promoted by the fascists from the mid-1920s onwards were simply the result of a period of social instability and political unrest directly following the First World War. The fanatical nationalism mixed with more than a hint of xenophobia which we now tend to associate with Mussolini's régime had in truth been growing for several decades and had already been evident in Italian foreign policy during the late 19th century. Even the so-called *Risorgimento*, a period which had seen the liberation of Italy from various foreign powers during the mid-1800s, had stirred up no small measure of heroic nationalism. And although Verdi's involvement in the newly born Republican movement has probably been exaggerated, his apparent disinterest, for example, in the music of Wagner together with his insistence on the necessity to 'rediscover' the true roots of Italian music are certainly symptomatic of sentiments prevalent in a good proportion of the population at the time.

As we have seen, at the beginning of the new century many composers, conductors, musicologists and critics began to take up Verdi's call to arms and did much to breathe new life into the music written by the Italian masters of the Renaissance and Baroque. But it was not only music that was caught up in such revivalism. A similar movement was, for example, also active in the world of literature and in 1919 the literary review *La Ronda* was founded by a group of writers, including Riccardo Bacchelli and Vincenzo Cardelli, with the aim of recapturing the spirit of the great Italian writers of the 16th century.

While the intentions of these groups were basically noble, in that they were reintroducing the public to works of high merit that had long been forgotten or ignored, there was always the danger that such intellectual themes would be translated into something more tangible. We have already seen how the Futurists (see Chapter Two) were part of an aesthetic movement that had tried to shock their audiences by their startlingly innovative approach to poetry, art and music. But the extremes expressed in their manifestos soon took on a truly political significance. Marinetti's famous *Manifesto* of October 1913, which was signed by a fair number of leading artists and musicians, includes, among other things, a call for all foreign 'interference' in Italian industry to be dispensed with immediately.

Sentiments such as these created no small dilemma for many composers, as it was clear to them that a total avoidance of foreign influence would inevitably lead to provincialism and even stagnation. We have already observed how many leading musicians had felt the necessity to spend some time outside of Italy to 'catch up' with the new ideas being developed elsewhere. Unfortunately, though, the authorities, and above all the general public, often failed to appreciate this point of view.

One of the first musical 'victims' of such chauvinism was Busoni, who had returned from abroad full of grand ideas about renewing the musical tradition of what he considered to be his own country. But after only two years, at the outbreak of the First World War, he was forced into what amounted to exile on account of his Germanic background. His place as the director of the Bologna Conservatory was, incidentally, taken over by the well established – and politically safer –   conductor and composer Gino Marinuzzi (1882 - 1945), who went on to be appointed as director of La Scala at the height of fascist rule.

The predilection for unadulterated, home-bred talent took on increasing significance as the régime became progressively more authoritarian. Although Italy was not wealthy enough to offer much financial support to its scientists – Marconi and Fermi were both forced to look elsewhere for funding – it had more than its fair share of first-class painters and musicians. Mussolini's 'talent scouts' were, for instance, quick to spot the prodigious talents of the young Bruno Maderna and, among other things, arranged for him to conduct a large orchestra in the grandiose setting of the Arena di Verona.

There is no denying, however, that right from its earliest years Fascism was much kinder to Italian composers who had long been established (almost exclusively composers of lyric opera) than to those of the new generation. Despite the fact that Musolini himself was keen to prove to the nation (and to the world at large) that he was not only a shrewd political leader but also a knowledgeable and would-be patron of the arts, his choice of composers whom he deemed fit to represent Italian culture throughout the world clearly betrays his partiality for recent tradition as opposed to any contemporary trends. Shortly after his rise to power he began to grant private hearings to a number of carefully selected composers in order to listen to their opinions and, more often than not, their grievances.

Among the first to be received by the Duce was Puccini, but the composer's insistence on wide-ranging reforms and state subsidies for the Italian theatre appear to have done little more than to irritate the leader.[1] Not long after, though, the composer was given full recognition for his services to Italian culture by being nominated as a senator in September 1924. But fate was to intervene, for he died in November of the same year before being fully sworn in.

Subsequently, after what had turned out to be an embarrassing interview with the priest composer Perosi,[2] Mussolini conceded a meeting with Mascagni. From 1923 onwards there ensued a long series of lively encounters and exchanges between the two strong-minded characters. Several years later, despite frequent clashes of personality, the composer was awarded one of the highest honours a musician could receive when he was elected as a member of the newly formed Accademia d'Italia.[3] Incidentally, Mascagni was joined on the board of the Accademia by Giordano, who was well past his peak, and in 1939 the same honour befell Cilea, who had not written

---

1 In due course, though, the state would take control of the management of La Scala as well as that of such important musical institutions as the Accademia di Santa Cecilia in Rome.

2 Apparently Perosi, then a highly esteemed figure in the musical world, used the meeting as an opportunity to pour out his doubts about his religious beliefs. He went so far as to confess his desire to become a protestant and move to Britain, something that Mussolini had not quite been expecting.

3 Mascagni, perhaps more than any other composer of his time, was determined to take advantage of the situation. It seems that he continuously begged for meetings with the Duce and failing that would send him letters and telegrams expressing his opinions and, more especially, trying to get his works performed. In the end it appears that he got much of his own way. Years after his death it came to light that

a successful opera for decades but whose opera *Andrea Lecouvreur* had seen a surprising revival in 1931.

For a government that had often declared its wish to foster and promote new talents the choice of these ageing 'veristi' was hardly an original one. The selection of Mascagni was taken quite badly by another composer, Alfano, who only two years before had had the great honour of having his second quartet performed not only in the presence of the country's leader, but actually in his personal residence. Officially he was highly esteemed as one of Italy's greatest living musicians and it goes without saying that the work in question received laudatory reviews. But the whole episode was obviously little more than a token gesture in the vague direction of modern instrumental music and had no lasting consequences.

The official music critics inevitably did much to reinforce and even exacerbate the situation. Bruno Barilli (1880 - 1952), for example, frequently expressed his opinion that the healthiest models for modern Italian music were to be found in the very 19th century lyric operas that many composers had been doing their best to forget. He even went so far as to insist on the superiority of Verdi's earlier works as compared to the later and technically more progressive *Otello* and *Falstaff*, whose innovations had, much to the critic's disdain, inspired much of the younger generation.

Needless to say, a fiercely anti-modernist stance was also taken by Alceo Toni (1884-1969), the critic of the fascist newspaper *Popolo d'Italia*. Interestingly, or perhaps typically, Toni had begun his career as a supporter and close friend of many of the Futurists (he was born in the same small town as Pratella, whose home had been a regular meeting place for advocates of the movement) but shortly after he started to speak out against the modern tendencies being adopted by many contemporary composers. This apparent contradiction once again highlights the embryonic 'fascism' that was creeping into many aspects of Italian society. Even the seemingly advanced ideals of the

in his old age he had received considerable sums of money from the state. But whether the payments were for his services to the régime or simply to pacify his flamboyant character we shall probably never know.

futurists were, like Mussolini's brand of fascism, grounded on a sort of progressively-minded conservatism.

Toni, incidentally, was a competent composer in his own right and also made a valuable contribution to the fashionable revival of ancient music by making piano and organ transcriptions of the works of forgotten composers like Vivaldi, Corelli and Pergolesi. Much of our present knowledge of Italian Renaissance and Baroque music, in fact, owes much to the work of genuine enthusiasts who were active during the years of Mussolini's rise to power. Yet the more strictly political proponents of New Italy were interested in another much more distant period, that of the golden age when ancient Rome had dominated the whole of the western world, an obsession that reached its peak in the 1930s, most ostensibly in Italian architecture.

Once again this cult was not entirely of fascist making. As far as music is concerned there is already evidence of 'Romanism' in works composed several years before Mussolini took power. In 1919 Puccini had written his *Inno a Roma* (Hymn to Rome), originally dedicated to Princess Jolanda of Savoy, but later taken up by the fascists and becoming the *Inno al Duce* (Hymn to the Duce). And Respighi, who in reality had never felt particularly at home in Rome, wrote a considerable number of pieces featuring and glorifying the city. He followed up the triumphal *Le Fontane di Roma* (1916) with *I Pini di Roma* (1924), which among other things concludes with a graphic musical representation of the Roman army marching triumphantly into the capital. And although Respighi's widow later suggested that the descriptive subtitles written in the score of this piece were added long after the composition, the music really speaks for itself[1].

Once the Roman theme had been made official there was, as can be imagined, a genuine proliferation of operas set in the ancient city or at least based on episodes relating to the Roman empire. The setting for what proved to be Respighi's most popular opera, *La Fiamma* (1934), is Ravenna, the city which had taken over from Rome as the capital of the western empire in 402 AD. Mascagni, on the other

---

1 See Elsa Respighi's biography of her late husband, *Ottorino Respighi* (trans. Gwyn Morris, Ricordi, London 1962).

hand, left no doubt as to his intentions when he chose the emperor Nero as the protagonist of his opera of the same name. Despite its blatant 'Romanism', which should, in theory, have acted as a guarantee for acceptance, if not success, the path of *Nerone* (1935) was by no means smooth. Plans to put on the first performance in Rome were continuously hindered and in the end the première took place at La Scala in Milan.[1]

The examples supplied by Respighi and Mascagni lead us to a rather complicated area of discussion. It would be far too simplistic to divide composers into those who were in favour of the régime and those who were against it. There were in reality a large number of composers who tolerated the hard line taken by the new government against modernity and in favour of popularism basically because they did not want to jeopardise their livelihood, that is, composition.

As far as figures like Mascagni were concerned they had everything to gain. After two decades of facing criticism and accusations of being old-fashioned, he was suddenly given a new lease of life. Likewise his contemporaries Giordano and Cilea underwent a sudden revival in popularity, while two slightly younger composers, Giuseppe Mulè (1885-1951) and Adriano Lualdi (1885-1971) both held various important cultural posts during the régime and found themselves in a privileged position that was totally disproportionate to their modest musical achievements. Their names would most likely have been forgotten had it not been for their overt adherence to Fascism.

During the early years of the régime various attempts were made to establish an official line as far as music and culture were concerned. In 1923 a group of musicians and critics, including Alfano, proposed the idea of organising a festival of modern Italian music. The project was accepted, but in the end the event, held in Bologna, turned out to be a disappointment. In 1925 the same city hosted a 'Congresso', basically a gathering of so-called intellectuals, which was chaired by the fascist philosopher Giovanni Gentile. The meeting led to the publication of a Manifesto setting out guidelines along which artists and

---

[1] At one point Mascagni even proposed the work should be premièred in the arena of the Coliseum.

musicians were expected to work, but once again the results were short-lived and after less than a year most of the decisions had been virtually forgotten.

A further move to give some sort of direction to fascist culture was made between 1928 and 1930 when the *Confederazione nazionale dei sindacati fasciti dei professionisti e degli artisti* (basically a national fascist union of musicians and artists) was set up. The honour of presiding over this body was given to Giuseppe Blanc, a staunch supporter of the régime and the composer of *Giovinezza*, the most popular official fascist anthem. Finally, a more lasting solution was found in 1935 with the creation of the *Ispettorato del Teatro* (a committee to supervise all forms of theatrical entertainment, including music), which was later to be incorporated into the wider-reaching *Ministero della Cultura Popolare* (whose guiding policy, as the name suggests, was to keep art at a popular level).

Against this background the careers of modern-minded composers like Casella and Malipiero, who had put so much effort into the renewal of Italian music, were potentially at risk. Until the mid-1920s they had been seen as representing the avant-garde of Italian music and had been accepted as such. But already during the first decade of fascism any references to non-Italian movements such as expressionism were being viewed with increasing suspicion. From the late 1920s onwards both composers were subject to attacks from critics who accused them of being élitist and anti-popularist. This attitude is summed up in the notorious anti-modernist manifesto published in two important national newspapers in December 1932, which was largely the work of Toni but was also signed by Respighi, Pizzetti, Zandonai and others[1]. At this point there was no longer any doubt as to the direction Italian music was taking.

The position taken by Casella remains somewhat unclear. Even while in France he had always wished to make his nationalistic sentiments known and one of his earliest successes was the *Rapsodia Italia* (1909) which concludes with a quite embarrassing rendition of the

---

[1] Alfano was among those who refused to put their names to the highly compromising document.

Neapolitan song *Funiculì funiculà*. Mention has already been made of his rather forced reference to Italian folklore, often in the form of movements entitled *Tarantella* or *Siciliano*, which appear in works he composed while still abroad. And although he had been an ardent promoter of the music of Mahler in Paris and later had even written essays virtually supporting the developments which were eventually to lead to the abandonment of tonality, his association with this essentially Germanic (and therefore non-Italian) movement never appears to have gone any further. Whether this was a direct result of political or social pressure to avoid 'contamination' from abroad, or merely a personal decision to favour simplicity as opposed to a more complex intellectual approach remains a question of debate. The fact remains that as far as experiments in tonality are concerned, the music he wrote during the years of the régime never ventures much beyond the occasional use of polytonality and a largely diatonic-based chromaticism.

Not long after Casella's involvement in the short-lived *Società Italiana di Musica Moderna* (1917-19) something in his attitude already appears to be changing. In an article published in 1924 entitled "*Arnold Schoenberg e la nuova Musica Italiana*"[1] he openly attacked the new tendencies emerging from abroad and practically negated the concept of atonality as a valid form of musical expression. Two years later he made his contribution to the 'Romanist' movement by calling his organ concerto the *Concerto Romano* (op.43, 1926), while the popular *Serenata* (1927-30) is generally much more light-hearted than his previous works and even manages to work another Neapolitan song into its otherwise sombre *Notturno*.

From the mid-1920s onwards, then, one cannot help but notice a certain restraint creeping into Casella's music. It is as if the natural line of his stylistic development, so ardently radical on his return from France, had suddenly been truncated. His output during the 1930s includes various large-scale works, but nothing that could be in anyway described as progressive. The *Concerto per violincello* (op.58,

---

[1] Published in the journal *Musica D'Oggi* (October 1924).

1934-35) is a pleasant and energetic piece notable for the delicate balance between the orchestra and soloist, but despite a certain amount of inventive chromaticism in its more reflective moments, it is on the whole a rather conservative piece, especially when compared to his earlier music. This tendency is even more noticeable in the *Sinfonia* written a few years later (op.63, 1939-40), which although based, like the concerto, on a basically classical structure, is meandering and at times even cumbersome.

Some commentators have suggested that Casella was suffering from a spiritual crisis during these years. And his uncomfortable position as a 'modernist' composer was compounded by the fact that his French wife was of Jewish origin. The unfavourable political and cultural climate of the time is clearly summed up in two articles published towards the end of the ′30s. In 1937 the composer and conductor Ennio Porrino (1910-1957) wrote of the need for "an art linked to our tradition..." guided by "...an instinctive repulsion towards tendencies of an international mark".[1] One month later the attack became decidedly more personal. In his notoriously outspoken article, Francesco Santoliquido spoke of Casella as a "prophet sent from Paris... with the precise task of conquering this great musical market in the name of the Jewish cause".[2]

Significantly, at the very moment when the twenty years of fascist rule (commonly referred to as the ventennio) was reaching its dramatic conclusion, Casella wrote what was to be his last orchestral piece, the *Concerto per Archi, Piano e Batteria* (op.69, 1943), which in many ways harks back to the more spirited style of works like *Puppazzetti* and, even more remarkably, makes a tentative use of two 12-note series in its first movement.

Malipiero, too, shows signs of reluctant resignation. His immediate response to the criticisms levelled against him in the 'anti-modernist' manifesto was to dedicate a collection of instrumental *Inni* (1932) to Mussolini and even though the fascist critic Toni remained unmoved and described the pieces as 'characterless', the point had nevertheless

---

[1] *Battaglie musicali* (Perseo, 15 November 1937).

[2] *La piovra musicale ebraica* (Il Tevere, 15 December 1937)

Gian Francesco Malipiero

been made. Significantly, the first of his eleven symphonies also dates from this period and even if there is no real sign of any conscious self-limitation, there is little doubt that Malipiero had decided to 'play it safe'.

Nonetheless there was yet another shock in store for him. In 1935 he collaborated with Pirandello in the writing of a new opera. The choice of his librettist should not, on the face of it, have presented any problems since the writer had openly supported the fascist movement for many years and had received several honours for his services to Italian literature. The work in question, *La Favola del Figlio Cambiato*, had its first performance in Germany and was at first well-received by the critics. But suddenly, after several performances it was banned. The German authorities had apparently decided that the plot contained subversive elements and that the music verged in places on atonality. As a direct consequence the work received only a single performance in Italy before being withdrawn from circulation by order of Mussolini. It appears that Malipiero was completely taken aback by this episode and was afraid, among other things, of losing his job at the *Liceo musicale* in Venice. It is surely no chance that his next two operas, *Giulio Cesare* (1936) and *Antonio e Cleopatra* (1938) both had an evident Roman theme.

No such dilemma appears to have presented itself to Pizzetti. Protected by the patriotic writer D'Annunzio and generally approved of by Toni he was never likely to find himself in the firing line of the anti-modernists. As far back as 1919 he had been accused of being too traditional by the then revolutionary Casella[1] and the two composers were again to clash over the withdrawal of the Italian contingent from the ranks of the International Society for Contemporary Music in 1923.

The truth is that right from the start Pizzetti's personal aesthetics were already remarkably close to those of the Fascist intellectuals: Italian music should be based on the noblest of sentiments, should aspire to the greatest of heights; it should have universal appeal, while still retaining a distinct national character. Like Mascagni he hated modern currents such as jazz and spoke out vehemently against Schoenberg and atonality. In 1931 he was awarded the *Premio Mussolini* (the Mussolini Award) for his opera *Dèbora e Jaéle*[2] and only at a later date, when the régime was beginning to tighten its reins, was he admonished for displaying a certain vagueness or ambiguity in his operas and was asked to base his work more on 'real life'. This led to a series of more subdued and perhaps less Pizzetian operas, beginning in 1935 with *Orsèolo*. Significantly, not long after the first performance of this less characteristic work the patriotic critic Luchini wrote: "The painting of Ottone Rosai is Fascist. The music of Ildebrando Pizzetti is Fascist"[3]

---

1 Ars Nova III (no.3, 1919).

2 An honour also bestowed upon Zandonai in 1935

3 Il Bargello (May 12th 1935).

Many other composers, especially those who were still completing their musical studies in the years immediately preceding fascism, suffered as a result of being, to all extents and purposes, cut off from the rest of the world. As a result we find composers like Lino Liviabella (1902-1964) sounding like a less bombastic version of Respighi, while Mario Castelnuovo-Tedesco (1895-1968) offers us a slightly more cheerful edition of his teacher Pizzetti.

It is here, alas, that we must begin to speak of those who truly suffered at the hands of the fascists, in particular during the later and harshest part of the régime, when Musolini was beginning to emulate, not always of his own choice, the actions and purges of Hitler. Castelnuovo-Tedesco could actually be counted among the most talented composers of his generation. His output was vast and of particular interest are his numerous works for guitar, which include a large number of solo pieces, two concertos (op.99, 1939; op.160, 1953) and various chamber works featuring the instrument. But as a Jew Castelnuovo-Tedesco was forced to leave Italy in 1939 and he subsequently settled down in the USA, where he lived and worked until his death.

A similar fate lay in store for many other musicians. Among these we find two pupils of Respighi, one of whom, Vittorio Rieti (1898-1994), also chose the USA for his exile, while his fellow-student and exact contemporary Renzo Massarani (1898-1975) eventually made his way to Brazil. More tragic was the destiny of Sinigaglia, who died in hospital while being arrested by the fascist police.

For some musicians the exile was to some extent self-imposed. Probably the most well-known 'fugitive' was Arturo Toscanini (1867-1957), whose motivation was probably more a question of principal and hurt pride than political harassment. He, like Puccini, had initially been attracted to the idea of the respectability, law and order offered by the new political movement. His name even appeared on the list of candidates for the fascist party in the 1919 elections, but as it turned out he was not elected.

We have already seen how the conductor's championship of certain Italian composers played no small part in their success at home and abroad and from this point of view his efforts should in theory have been appreciated by the fascists. One of his favourite contemporary operas was, in fact, Pizzetti's *Dèbora e Jaéle*, the very work that was later to earn the composer official recognition.However, Toscanini was a highly-strung character and was easily offended. On several occasions he refused to comply with the formality of beginning concerts with the fascist anthems and the situation came to a head in 1931 when he was asked if he intended to play the anthem *Giovinezza* at the Martucci memorial concerts to be held in Bologna. He immediately lost his calm and replied that such pieces were not in keeping with the tone of his programme. The struggle that ensued led to the conductor being struck and his consequent withdrawal first to his hotel and then, soon afterwards, to the USA. Despite numerous invitations and much beseeching, he did not return to conduct in Italy until the occasion of the historical re-opening of La Scala after the war in May 1946.

Mention should also be made of the many intellectuals, who, during the 1930s, took a firm stand against what was being imposed upon them and suffered as a result. As a reaction against the well-meaning, but essentially over-patriotic literary movements belonging to the early years of fascism a group of Italian writers, including such important names as Cesare Pavese, began to look towards the free-thinking American authors for their inspiration. As the demands of the régime grew increasingly more severe Pavese, together with the publisher Giulio Einaudi, was arrested, while other writers such as Carlo Levi were 'exiled' to the south of Italy for their outspoken views. Also involved in the movement was the highly acclaimed musicologist and critic Massimo Mila (1910-1988) who had already been arrested at the age of 19 for his participation in anti-fascist activities and later spent five years (1935-40) in prison.

Despite this rather dismal chronicle it could be argued that some good did actually come out of this otherwise controversial period of Italian history, at least from an organisational point of view. During the first two decades of the century important institutions such as music conservatories and opera houses had been suffering from neglect and mismanagement and were therefore in sore need of reform. The intervention of the state in the 1920s and '30s, although involving the inevitable appointment of fascist sympathisers in key positions, could nonetheless be said to have been timely. Moreover, the publication of the authoritative *Enciclopedia Treccani* (first compiled 1929-37 and still the most respected Italian encyclopaedia after almost a century) owes its inspiration to an industrialist of the same name who was encouraged and supported by the Ministry of Culture. The task of overseeing the music section of the encyclopaedia was, incidentally, given to Pizzetti, providing further evidence of the esteem the composer enjoyed at the time.

Finally, the real influence and negative effects of the 'popularist' and 'anti-modernist' schools should not be over-exaggerated. During the 1930s several important festivals were established, some with the specific aim of encouraging and promoting new music. Among these were the *Festival di Venezia* (1930), the *Maggio Musicale Fiorentino* (1933) and the *Settimana Musicale Senese* (organised by Casella and founded in 1939). Not only did these festivals give the public the opportunity (which would otherwise have been considerably limited) to hear works by leading foreign composers like Bartók and Stravinsky, but the new wave of young Italian composers were given a rare chance to display their wares in public.

We might conclude, then, that unlike other countries that were also subjected to a period of authoritarian rule, Italy did not undergo a total suffocation of artistic freedom at the hands of the régime. The proposed establishment (and source of much discussion) of a set of idealised rules to 'guide' artistic creation was certainly evidence of the government's restrictive intentions. But it should not be forgotten that one of the saving qualities of modern Italians is that their rules are so often left open to interpretation.

5

TOWARDS A MODERN IDIOM

The years surrounding the Second World War saw a veritable exodus of composers and musicians from Europe. Most of them, including Bartók, Hindemith and Schoenberg, headed for the security of the USA. In Italy, however, apart from the handful of names mentioned in the previous chapter, the cultural drain was surprisingly limited.

If the effects of fascist authoritarianism were, at least from a musical point of view, not so drastic as one might have expected, this was largely thanks to the careful and intelligent handling of the situation by certain prominent figures working within the organs of the state, who were, all things considered, given a fairly free hand in making their choices. One such person was Mario Labroca (1896-1973), a pupil of Respighi and Malipiero and himself an established composer. In the early 1920s he had worked alongside Casella and others with the common purpose of promoting new music in Italy. During the years of the régime he was given a series of important positions on various cultural boards and committees and it was thanks to his involvement in the *Maggio Musicale Fiorentino* that the livelihood of many contemporary composers was safeguarded.

Evidence that the decisions taken by people like Labroca were based on sound personal judgement and not on any dictates from above comes, for example, from the fact that he bluntly refused to accept a revival of Pratella's opera *L'Aviatore Dro* (see Chapter 2), which he considered nothing more than "a work of exasperating amateurism". What is more, his decision stood despite the insistence of such an in-

fluential and highly favoured writer as Marinetti, the spiritual leader
of the futurist movement and a close friend of Pratella. And the fact
that after the collapse of fascism Labroca continued to work in such
important institutions as La Fenice in Venice and La Scala in Milan
is surely proof of his genuine organisational skill and, more to the
point, of his political impartiality.

Giorgio Federico Ghedini

And so it was that in the programmes of the *Maggio musicale* and other festivals, as well as in those of the major opera houses, we begin to find composers belonging to a completely new generation whose work continues along the progressive line established in the early 1920s by Casella, Malipiero and others. Although most of the new 'school' were born in the first years of the new century, the process of renewal is already apparent in the music of Giorgio Federico Ghedini (1892-1965), who, like Malipiero, spent a brief but profitable period of study in the capable hands of M.E.Bossi.

Under his teacher's guidance Ghedini soon became caught up in the revival of the Italian Renaissance and Baroque with the result that much of his earlier work is tinted with the hues of ancient modes, a tendency that was to re-emerge unexpectedly towards the end of his career. But apart from the use of modes, the greatest influence of early music on Ghedini's music is reflected in his choice of form. Right from his first important work, the *Partita per orchestra* (1926), he consistently turned to typically Baroque structures and was much indebted to the characteristic episodic structure of the concerto grosso. The systematic contraposition of different instrumental groups is, in fact, one of the most distinctive features of Ghedini's mature style.

What singles him out from his contemporaries, though, is the way his own personal style seems to have developed steadily throughout his career without being hindered or in any way limited by the cultural climate prevailing at the time. During what is generally referred to as his middle period (roughly speaking from 1940-48) he was not afraid to show how he had fully absorbed the idioms of non-Italian composers like Bartók and Stravinsky and even went so far as to dabble with atonality. His music of this period is marked by a strong use of dissonance coupled with energetic rhythms, very evident in works like *Architetture* (1940) or in the *7 Ricercari* for violin, cello and piano (1945). These elements are again combined in what is probably his best known work, the *Concerto dell'albatro* (1945), where two instrumental groups, a string trio and piano on the one hand and an orchestra on the other, are set against each other in a way that strongly recalls Baroque usage. The eerie atmosphere pervading this piece reaches its height in the concluding part of the work where a voice recites an extract from Melville's *Moby Dick* against a sparse instrumentation evoking the bitter cold of the Antarctic.

Towards the end of his life Ghedini appears to have become more meditative and even a little conservative. This is already noticeable in his concerto for two cellos and orchestra known as *L'Olmenata* (1951), where the general mood is one of relaxed contemplation, something that was to characterise much of his later works. From the mid-1950s onwards his music begins to lose much of its neo-classical verve and also shows a marked return to traditional tonality. In comparison to the earlier *7 Ricercari* a work like the second *Quartetto per archi* (1959) seems to have lost its jagged edges and forgotten the emotional force of dissonance. This apparent turnabout is quite curious at a moment in history when, as we shall see, most Italian composers were eagerly taking advantage of their newly gained artistic freedom and the extraordinary opportunities created by new technology.

In contrast, no after-thoughts appear to have disturbed the resolve of AntonioVeretti (1900-1978), a composer who towards the end of his career went steadfastly in the direction of dodecaphony and never looked back. His early operas *Il medico volante* (1923-24 on a libretto by the neo-classical writer Bacchelli) and *Il favorito del Re* (1932) clearly embrace the theatrical reforms of Pizzetti, while the *Duo Strumentale* (1925) and other instrumental works of the 1920s and early 1930s adopt a Casella-like form of neo-classicism. His collaboration with the régime in writing the scores for such films as *L'Assedio dell'Alcazar* (1940), one of the many patriotic films being produced at the recently built state-of-the-arts studios known as *Cinecittà*, might be interpreted as just a momentary lapsus, for as soon as the Second World War was over he was quick to resume his quest for modernity. During the 1950s he passed through an initial period of experimentation with dodecaphonic techniques in works like the opera-ballet *I Sette Peccati* (1956) until finally reaching his own personal interpretation of total serialism in his last works.

Two composers of the same generation who adopted a decidedly more conservative approach were Mario Pilati (1903-1938) and

Salviucci (second left), Casella (fifth left), Petrassi (sixth left)

Giovanni Salviucci (1907-37). Both died at a tragically early age and there is, of course, no way of knowing how their style may have evolved had they lived longer. The extent of Pilati's recognition can be deduced from the fact that in 1926 he was awarded the Elizabeth Coolidge Prize of $1,000 for his Sonata for flute and piano, an honour also bestowed on Bartok, Stravinsky and Schoenberg. The Sonata was written when the composer was still young, but displays a striking affinity with the chamber works of Ravel. Another interesting piece by Pilati is the stylistically unadventurous, but still enjoyable *Concerto in Do maggiore per pianoforte e orchestra* (1932).

While Pilati tended towards French impressionism, the relatively small amount of music left to us by Salviucci shows a distinctly neo-romantic bent. He studied under Respighi in Rome and inherited much of his teacher's love for orchestral colour, although this influence was mellowed to a certain extent by his previous studies with the Roman organist and conductor Ernesto Boezi (1856-1946) who had instilled in him a keen interest in Renaissance polyphony. But the majority of his mature works are full of the extravagant outbursts commonly associated with the music of Respighi and it is no surprise that among his works we find several symphonic poems and even a contribution to the 'Roman eulogy' in the suite *Campagna Romana* (1931).

Towards the end of his brief life a gradual move away from traditional tonality began to emerge. Certain passages from the *Introduzione, Passacaglia e finale* (1934) have often been singled out as representing this new direction, while the trend becomes even more marked in the more intimate *Serenata per 9 strumenti* (1937), first performed a few days after his death during the *Festival di Venezia*. Contemporary critics were unanimous in heralding Salviucci as one of the most promising figures of the new generation, frequently placing his name alongside those of Dallapiccola and Petrassi, and one cannot help but wonder where this new path might have led had time been more generous to the composer.

Luigi Dallapiccola (1904-75) had the distinct advantage of having been born in Istria, which at that time was still under Austrian rule. This particular geographical situation meant that from an early age he was exposed to three very different cultures, namely, Italian, Austrian and Slovenian. This multicultural background enabled him overcome the barriers of Italian provincialism and it is surely no chance that he was one of the few composers to have fully appreciated the true significance of the thoughts and achievements of Busoni[1].

In many ways Dallapiccola could be said to represent the bridge between the old and the new in Italian music. For although he was one of the first Italians to make consistent use of the dodecaphonic technique, echoes of the lyricism of Puccini may also been heard in some of his operas. And while he showed great interest in the revival of early Italian music, he felt no aversion towards the romanticism of the late 19th century. Dallapiccola frequently acknowledged the fundamental importance of Verdi in his musical formation and his exposure to Germanic culture in his youth and early career had also led him to admire the works of Wagner and Mahler.

---

[1] He and his wife translated many of Busoni's letters and other writings into Italian.

Luigi Dallapiccola

He was therefore one of the most eclectic Italian composers of his time and drew much inspiration from the music he heard during his many trips abroad. Strains of Ravel filter through the transparent score of the *Piccolo Concerto per Muriel Couvreux* for piano and chamber orchestra (1941), while the percussiveness of the *Due Studi per Violino e Pianoforte* (1946-7) is almost Bartokian. And yet despite his decidedly international outlook he also played his part in the revival of the Italian baroque and paid homage to Tartini in two works for orchestra and violin that he called *Tartiniana* (1951) and *Tartiniana Seconda* (1956), as well as paying a novel tribute to another Italian genius in the *Sonatina Canonica* for piano (1942-43), where a set of variations on a theme by Paganini is cleverly arranged to comply with the canons of serialism.

Dallapiccola's first important composition, the *Partita* for soprano and orchestra (1930-32), was given its first performance in 1933 during the somewhat uncomfortable period when other composers were being criticised for their ultra-modern tendencies. It was nevertheless during this very period that his interest in new compositional techniques began to develop. An experimental use of 12-note rows first appears in his opera *Volo di Notte* (1939-1940), a piece inspired by the work of the French writer Saint-Exupéry, whom he had met during his visit to Paris in 1937. The opera, like the original novel, is largely a meditation on solitude, freedom and destiny, themes that were to recur in many of his mature works.

His experiments in serialism continued in the *Canti di Prigionia* (1938-42) and were consolidated in the *Liriche Greche* (1942-5). He was particularly fascinated by the new opportunities that the technique offered to polyphony, something he had long admired in the music of Italian masters such as Monteverdi and Gesualdo. In his hands the intricate network of polyphonic writing took on a whole new meaning and the combination of the Gregorian *Dies Irae* and a twelve-note row in the *Canti di Prigionia* is surely a supreme moment not only in the music of Dallapiccola, but also in the development of modern music in Italy. For the first time the simplicity of Renaissance art and the complexities of 20th century expressionism are perfectly blended without producing any sense of cultural or stylistic clash. Remarkable too is the blatant cry for freedom emanating from the texts of these works at a time when racial persecution was reaching its height in Italy.

Once again the government's mute acceptance of such an explosive mixture of modernity and libertarianism might be seen as evidence of how Italian fascism was, all things considered, more tolerant than the régimes at work in Germany or Russia. In a more rigid climate of censorship Dallapiccola would almost certainly have been ostracised and probably forced to leave the country.[1] The importance of having such a national genius in Italy appears to have outweighed any potentially damaging action. His works were promoted at festivals such as the *Maggio Musicale Fiorentino* and in 1939 the fascist minister Bottai

---

[1] Under pressure from Hitler, the fundamentally anti-semitic Racial Law was issued in Italy on 14 July 1938. When Italy was definitively invaded by the German army in 1943 Dallapiccola was forced to retire to a country villa near Fiesole with his wife Laura, who was of Jewish origin.

rewarded him for his services by offering him a professorship at the Florence Conservatory.

The theme of freedom in the works of Dallapiccola was to persist long after the Second World War had ended. His second opera *Il Prigionere* (1949), for example, is a drama involving the plight of a prisoner who believes he has escaped, only to be caught and escorted back to his execution. Although serial techniques are again applied in this work, there are also intermittent references to traditional tonality, a feature that makes the work more accessible and aligns it with the more lyrical approach adopted by Schoenberg's pupil Alban Berg. However, in the following decade his use of serialism became increasingly more systematic, culminating in the complex *Canti di Liberazione* (1953-55), where once more the question of liberty resurfaces.

Dallapiccola's repeated allusion to freedom was without doubt closely linked to his profound religious beliefs. The unquestioning acceptance of the 'mystery' required by the Catholic faith led him to become almost obsessed with certain issues, including the apparent conflict between freedom of choice and destiny. This passion for the truth, together with his love of Greek literature and mythology, where the intervention and acceptance of fate plays a key role, provided the psychological background for many of the works he wrote during the 1950s and 60s. For example, he composed a 'sacred representation' based on the biblical story of *Job* (1950), whose acceptance of destiny led to his destruction and salvation, and the same theme pervades his final opera *Ulisse* (1968), a work that the composer considered as his masterpiece, but that has yet to meet critical acclaim.

The other leading composer of the period was Goffredo Petrassi (1904- 2003), a greatly respected and remarkably long-lived composer who virtually saw the passing of the whole twentieth century. He was born in exactly the same year as Dallapiccola and even though his origins were of a much humbler kind, it is only to be expected that the two composers should have certain things in common. The ubiquitous figure of Verdi, for instance, can once again be found lurking in the composer's background, even though in the case of Petrassi it was more a question of admiration than direct influence. Unlike

Dallapiccola, his theatrical output was quite insubstantial and was limited to a brief phase during the 1940s that saw the composition, among other things, of two unassuming operas.

Petrassi's apparent lack of ambition as far as musical theatre is concerned does not mean that vocal music did not play an important part in his music. Many of his earlier works, including the setting of *Psalm IX* (1934-36) and the *Magnificat* (1939-40), bear witness to his interest in the 16th century polyphonic tradition and this, combined with his strong religious and mystic sentiments, was something that remained fundamental to the numerous choral works written throughout his long career. A fine example of Petrassian polyphony can be heard in the bleak strains of the 'mystic cantata' *Noche Oscura* (1950) where the vocal and orchestral lines mingle to form a single, homogeneous texture.

As was the case with both Ghedini and Dallapiccola, the first work to bring Petrassi national and international acclaim was a *Partita for orchestra* (1933). This seeming coincidence can actually be explained by the fact that in the early 1930s the Italian state was already refusing to accept foreign nomenclatures, including the French term 'suite', and so the choice of title for a collection of classically inspired dance movements was consequently rather limited. The unexpected success of the *Partita* was an important turning point in Petrassi's career, as it spurred him on to write the first of what was to be a series of concertos for orchestra that take us right through his main creative periods.

Both the *Partita* and the *Concerto per Orchestra* (1934), the first of eight such concertos, belong to what might be referred to as Petrassi's neo-classical phase. The typical use of tonality with modal inflections and the harmonic progressions reminiscent of Hindemith are features common to much Italian music of the time. On the other hand, certain aspects that were soon to become hallmarks of Petrassi's individual style are already discernible in these works, above all the characteristic dynamism and rhythmic vitality.

His second *Concerto per orchestra* (1951) did not appear until the early 1950s when the composer was just beginning to make tentative moves away from tonality. This transition towards a more chromatic

Goffredo Petrassi

Petrassi (right) with Elliott Carter

and less diatonic idiom can quite clearly be perceived by comparing this second Concerto, still firmly rooted in the tonal tradition, with the sixth (1957), where a decisive step is taken in the direction of serialism.[1]

Petrassi's first openly serial work is generally considered to be his *Quartetto* (1958) even though his application of the technique is still very much a personal affair. The intervals chosen for the series are carefully thought out and it is always the composer's creative intent that dominates the scheme and never *vice versa*. His feelings about giving in to the latest fashion were neatly summed up many years later in an interview in which the composer reminisces about his first approaches to the system: "When I went to the conference on dodecaphony which had been organised in Milan by Malipiero and Dallapiccola [the *Congresso di Dodecafonia*, 1949] I was like a poor relation, an outsider, because they were the trustees of a truth that I did not yet possess."

Although some commentators have pointed out a passing reference to indeterminacy in the final cadenza of his *Concerto per flauto* (1960), Petrassi never showed any real enthusiasm about such avant-garde techniques. In the end he did not even go as far as Dallapiccola in his adoption of dodecaphony and did not seem to be attracted to the more rigid applications being proposed by the Webernian school of thought. Strong elements of rudimentary serialism still appear in the last two concertos for orchestra (1964, 1972), but again in a form very much tailored to the needs of the composer, who always felt strongly about the importance of individual creative choice. Both of these concertos, written at the beginning of what was to be his final creative phase, are characterised by a harsh and almost aggressive use of dissonance, accentuated by prominent brass and percussion sections. Themes, in the broadest sense of the term, tend to be made up of rhythmic motifs and sections of contrasting textures as opposed to any recognisable sequences of notes, but although tonality is generally avoided, it is not altogether excluded.

---

[1] Hints of serialism can already be heard in *Noche Oscura*, written a year before the second concerto for orchestra.

In many of Petrassi's very last works, written in the years immediately before he was forced to abandon composition due to his failing eye-sight, snatches of tonal-based melody are not uncommon and one can clearly sense a melting down of the former harshness that had characterised much of his mature work. This is already noticeable in the *Grand Septuor* (1977) and becomes even more evident in the *Sestina d'Autunno "Veni creator Igor"* (1981-82), where any sense of anger or aggression has given way to a more delicate touch set against lighter and generally more transparent textures.

Petrassi's relationship with the régime was in many ways a question of convenience. His music, like that of Dallapiccola, was widely promoted during the fascist period and he was very much involved in the decision-making for concert programmes. He was actually one of three young composers appointed to the official body known as the *Ispettorato del Teatro* and he later held an important position as the superintendent of La Fenice in Venice. And yet the suffering brought about by the war (and by the régime) left Petrassi deeply moved. On hearing the tragic declaration of war against France in 1940 he felt he should express his feelings by writing a piece that he described as a 'reaction', but which in reality was nothing less than a protest. The result was one of his best known choral works, the *Coro dei Morti*, first performed in 1942 while the war was still very much in progress. In setting the text by the 19th century Italian poet Leopardi, the composer deliberately avoided the gentler sonority of strings and woodwind and chose to use a male-voice choir accompanied by a chamber ensemble of three pianos, brass and percussion.

Apart from his achievements as a composer Petrassi will also be remembered for his long career as a skilled and much-loved teacher. During the years he spent teaching composition in Rome, first at the Conservatory and later at the Academy, he guided and inspired a whole generation of younger composers, not only Italians (Morricone, Clementi, Ferrero, Gentile, to name but a few) but also numerous foreign visitors, including the British composers Peter Maxwell Davies and Cornelius Cardew. He was also in great demand abroad, especially for summer schools like Tanglewood in the USA where he held a composition course in 1956.

Petrassi's generation was beginning to be attracted (mostly for the immediate financial rewards on offer) by a relatively new field, that of writing film scores for the booming Italian film industry. Petrassi himself wrote the music for several films by such illustrious directors as De Santis and Zurlini, but the restrictions imposed by the genre offered him little creative satisfaction. His big moment could actually have arrived in the mid-sixties when he was commissioned to write the score for Huston's colossal *The Bible*. Unfortunately, the director was not impressed by what he heard and the whole project was abandoned.

The art of writing for the cinema eventually became something of a speciality among the Italians. One of the best loved film composers of all times was Nino Rota (1911-1979), who not only worked with the greatest Italian directors of the post-war period (including Visconti, Zeffirelli and, above all, Fellini), but also met with international acclaim when he won an Oscar for the music he wrote for Coppola's *The Godfather*. Rota's output was, however, by no means limited to the cinema. His catalogue also includes five symphonies, numerous concertos for a wide variety of instruments (including an interesting double bass concerto, 1969) and a fair amount of chamber music.

Unlike the majority of composers of his time Rota showed little or no inclination to follow the modernist tendencies that were dominating the music of the 1950s and '60s. Apart from the occasional use of 'fashionable' neo-classical forms, as can be seen in the *Sarabanda e Toccata per Arpa* (1945), he displayed no desire to adhere to any particular school or movement. A certain influence inevitably resulted from his friendship with Stravinsky, but this never amounts to much more than the momentary use of irregular rhythmic motifs or snatches of bitonality, something he often used to add an element of irony to a particular passage. Both features are well-displayed in the opening bars of the *Trio per flauto, violino e pianoforte* (1958), where ragged violin chords accompany the soaring flute line. As in the majority of such cases, though, any apparent 'modernity' in Rota's music soon gives way to an exhibition of unashamed romanticism often featuring sweeping melodies that seem to hark back to the beginning of the century and beyond.

In reality, the remarkable simplicity achieved by Rota should not be read merely as a sign of nostalgia for the past. On the contrary, it could be seen as a very personal interpretation of the present, something to be admired at a time marked by conflict and change. During a tribute to Rota a few years after his death[1] the critic Fedele D'Amico underlined the 'spontaneity' and 'immediacy' of his music, two words that seem particularly apt.

This directness again features prominently in Rota's numerous operas and it is perhaps on this account that while similar works by his contemporaries have only been sporadically revived, regular performances of his two most successful operas, *Il Cappello di Paglia di Firenze* (1944/5, first perf. 1955) and *La Notte di un Nevrastenico* (1959), have continued well into the 21st century. It would perhaps be an overgeneralization to say that audiences towards the end of the 20th century were beginning to tire of the extreme experimental nature of much of what had been written after the Second World War. Yet looking back, it was almost as if Rota, without knowing it, had been the forerunner of a later generation of composers who were to rediscover the simple, but disregarded value of speaking directly to their public.

The same might be said of Gian Carlo Menotti (1911-2007) were it not for the fact that his works cannot always be described as uncomplicated in their emotional demands. And one also has the impression that his was not a rediscovery of simplicity but rather a somewhat forced prolongation of verismo opera. His notable success was very much a question of circumstances. While still in his teens he took Toscanini's advice and moved to the USA, a country without any real operatic tradition and where Italian lyric opera had always been welcomed with open arms (and hearts) by the vast numbers of Italian immigrants residing in cities like New York.

At his best Menotti was able to recapture the lightness and melodic

---

1 Pistoia 1981

charm of the less dramatic 'veristi'. These features are used to good effect in the opera *Amahl and the Night Visitors* (1951), a work originally commissioned for American television and therefore aimed at a particular type of mass audience. His other more 'serious' operas, including *The Consul* (1950) and *The Saint of Bleeker Street* (1954), tend to drown in their own melodrama and although they occasionally borrow rhythms or instrumental effects from jazz they offer very little in the way of inventiveness.

His greatest achievement was probably the establishment, in 1958, of the Spoleto Festival, an annual event also known as the 'Festival of Two Worlds' since it offers a chance for young European and American composers to come together and make music in the beautiful setting of the Umbrian countryside. Menotti, incidentally, took advantage of his position as the director of the festival by opening the 2001 edition with a revival of *The Saint of Bleeker Street*, a work that would otherwise have remained buried in the archives. Interestingly, it was this very work that led the musicologist Joseph Kerman to condemn the composer as "a sensationalist in the old style, and in fact a weak one, diluting the faults of Strauss and Puccini with none of their fugitive virtues."[1]

Although the 1950s probably saw the last spate of traditionally conceived operas that met with any great or immediate success, the lure of romantic opera was reluctant to fade. Apart from the works written in this period by Rota and Menotti many other composers produced well received (but soon forgotten) theatrical pieces. Among these the names of Vieri Tosatti (1920-1999) and Luciano Chailly (1920-2002) stand out. Tosatti, a pupil of Pizzetti and later of Petrassi, might well be referred to as one of the last of the great Wagnerites and curiously he chose the late 1950s to be 'converted', a time when most of the musical world was trying to forget the dramatic and emotional excesses of the recent past. Chailly, on the other hand, will probably be remembered not so much for his operas, which include the *Ferrovia Sopraelevata* (1955) and *Il Mantello* (1960), both written in col-

---

1 In his book *Opera as Drama* (New York 1956, 1962)

laboration with the then fashionable writer Dino Buzzati, but above all for his involvement in the promotional and organisational side of the genre. In addition to his long association with Italian television and radio he was also the artistic director of several important opera venues including La Scala and the Arena di Verona[1]

To be fair to Chailly the idiom he adopted was a long way from the 'diluted Strauss and Puccini' of Menotti and others. His studies with Hindemith in the late '40s had a strong influence on the music he wrote during the following decade and he even ventured an occasional foray into the world of serialism and atonality. In his numerous vocal and orchestral works that spanned the last part of the century he went on to develop his own personal approach to post-war modernity without allowing himself to be caught up in the powerful wind of change that, as we shall see, was sweeping across the whole of Europe.

---

1 The name Chailly is now more often associated with the composer's son Riccardo, who became one of the most celebrated conductors of the end of the century.

6

DARMSTADT AND BEYOND

In the years following the end of the Second World War the prevalent desire throughout Europe was to turn over a new leaf and start afresh. Italy in particular had every reason to want to forget recent events and look to the future with an open mind.

This was the moment that many writers and intellectuals had been waiting for. The mid-1940s saw the publication of a series of important literary works offering fresh insight into life during the long period of fascist rule. Carlo Levi's *Cristo si è fermato a Eboli* (1945), based on his experience of political exile, soon became a classic and was later made into a film by the neo-realist director Francesco Rosi. A year later Carlo Emilio Gadda published his experimental novel *Quer pasticciaccia brutto de via Merulana* in instalments in the literary journal *Letteratura*. And in 1947 Italo Calvino, probably the best known Italian writer of the 20th century and important also for his collaboration with composers such as Luciano Berio, published his first novel *Il sentiero dei nidi di ragno*, a tale of the Italian resistance and its struggle against the régime.

And yet the opportunity to create a free state where writers, artists and musicians could finally express themselves without fear of censorship, or at least strong criticism, was in reality only partially realised, for in the years immediately following the historical referendum in 1946, which saw the defeat of the monarchists and the setting up of a new republic, Italian politics took a sudden and unexpected turn. Instead of uniting forces to create a truly liberal state the formerly solid anti-fascist groups were destined to split over the question of communism, a situation directly linked to the beginning of the Cold War with the Soviet Union and possibly fuelled by American interventionship. As a result many of the much-hoped-for social and economic reforms were delayed or blocked by what turned out to be a parliament afraid of giving too much power to the Partito Comunista Italiano, which since its foundation in 1921 had never had so much open support as it did now. Ironically it was the Italian communists, more than any other political movement of the post-war years, who had a decisive influence on the artistic and intellectual climate of the time.

As far as music was concerned Italian composers were doubtlessly much freer to make their individual creative choices. But due to the uncertain and basically conservative political climate of the late 1940s and early '50s they were once again forced to look abroad for encouragement and support. By far the most important centre for innovation in post-war Europe was the German town of Darmstadt. Originally founded in 1946 to regenerate German musical invention, the annual summer course became international in 1948 and went on to attract the most important composers of the age, including Messiaen, Boulez, Stockhausen and Cage, to mention but a few.

The Darmstadt courses offered Italian composers undreamed-of opportunities to show the rest of the world what their country had to offer. And even though Petrassi, one of the greatest and internationally well-known Italian composers from this period, decided to turn down an invitation to participate in the courses, convinced as he was that he had very little to offer the new avant-garde, the younger generation was quick to take up the challenge.

During the relatively brief period when the 'Darmstadt effect' was at its height, the turnover of new musical ideas was extraordinarily rapid. At first the main focus of attention was the dodecaphonic heritage left by Schoenberg and more especially the more rigorous application of the technique developed by Webern, but this soon evolved into a form generally referred to as 'total serialism' where every aspect of the music (including structure, rhythm, dynamics and even tone colour) was strictly dependent on the basic numerical series. Towards the end of the '50s this too began to give way to a European brand of 'aleatory' music or indeterminacy, an approach that to a large extent left the form of a piece to the choice of the performer or, in some cases, to pure chance.

The elements of structural freedom that were incorporated into Stockhausen's *Klavierstuck XI* (1956) and Boulez's *Third Piano Sonata* (1956-57) in many ways represented a turning point in the importance of the Darmstadt courses. The solidarity and optimism which had characterised the meetings for almost a decade was finally disrupted by the arrival of the American composer John Cage in 1958, whose virtually nihilistic attitude towards composition left many participators perplexed and eventually led to a conflict of ideals. His extreme use of chance, coupled with the novel and often eccentric involvement of the performer in the composition attracted some composers but left doubts in the minds of many others.

The Italian contingent at Darmstadt during the 1950s was particularly active. One of the first regular participants was Camillo Togni (1922-93), a pupil of Casella and, despite his teacher's outspoken attacks against serialism in the 1920s, a convinced advocate of the system. The influence of Schoenberg can already be seen in the 7 *Serenate* written in the early 1940s and his use of serialism as a compositional technique gradually evolved until being definitively sealed by his experiences in the summer courses. He was particularly attracted by the intimacy offered by small-scale chamber and vocal works and was often inspired by German texts, especially those of the writer Geog Trakl, whose work had already been set to music by Webern (e.g. in the 6 *Lieder* op. 14). Written ostensibly under the influence of Webern, the 5 *Lieder, Helian di Trakt* (1955) are among the most representative of Togni's works, while the opera *Blaubart* (1975), again on a text by Trakl, may appear to be an uncharacteristic excursion into the grander world of the theatre, but is in reality a highly condensed expressionist opera lasting no more than half an hour.

It was, however, the work of another Italian composer that aroused the enthusiasm of the Darmstadt group. Luigi Nono (1924-90) imme-

Camillo Togni

diately made his mark with the performance of *Polifonica-Monodia-Ritmica* (1951), a piece that was acclaimed as one of the first to capture the essence of 'Neue Musik'.[1] With its extreme fragmentation and sparseness of texture, the work offers a fine example of what has come to be known as musical 'pointillism' and as such typified the new form of expression the group was aspiring towards in its earliest years.

---

1 Neue Musik has been defined as "… a term, almost a slogan, to indicate music that was not merely new but avant-garde" (Paul Griffiths, *Encyclopaedia of 20th century Music*, Thames and Hudson, 1992).

The Venetian composer's approach to serialism largely derived from his contact with Herman Scherchen, the German composer, conductor and champion of the new Viennese school. Nono had first embraced the precepts of serialism in his *Variazioni Canoniche* (1950), which is actually based on the note-row used in Schoenberg's *Ode to Napoleon*, and his association with the founder of dodecaphony was further consolidated by his marriage to Schoenberg's daughter Nuria in 1955. But Nono was soon to become disillusioned with the limitations imposed by the strict application of this system and as early as 1955 in the *Canto Sospeso* (1955-56) we can recognise a new tendency where the music is allowed to develop more freely, evolving from the basic nature of the sound itself.

The *Canto Sospeso*, a choral work based on fragments taken from letters written by various members of the European Resistance who had been condemned to death during the Second World War, also marks the beginning of the political activism that was to become the hallmark of much of Nono's later work. His left-wing ideals, together with a strong sense of humanitarianism, eventually led him away from the mainstream of the avant-garde. He began to regard the passive adherence to a set of preconceived rules, or the abandonment of the music to the vagaries of chance, as a severe restriction of creative liberty. Even in earlier works such as the *España en el corazon* (1952), dedicated to the memory of the Spanish poet Garcia Lorca, the need to give rein to a more personal form of emotional expression is already evident and an underlying lyricism, absent from many other exponents of the avant-garde, can be detected behind the general harshness of the music.

Such hints of lyricism could in fact be said to link Nono not only with the mainstream of Italian tradition but also with the late-romanticism from which the new Viennese school had originally developed. The combination of this strong need for freedom of expression and a profound interest in the human condition become increasingly marked in works written towards the end of the 1950s. In the politically inspired *Composizione no 2 - Diario polacca '58* (1959) the tragedy of authoritarian oppression finds its musical expression in moments of quiet contemplation that are rudely interrupted by strident cries on the brass.

The composition of *Intolleranza* (1960) represents a landmark in Nono's career, and also in the history of Italian musical theatre. The linguistic innovations previously introduced in *Il Canto Sospeso*, where words were reduced to syllables and syllables to phonemes, are now applied within a theatrical context. To call *Intolleranza* an opera would be something of a misnomer, for although a rudimental story runs through the work, telling the universal tale of a worker trying to escape from exploitation and persecution, the action on stage is not continuous but consists of a juxtaposition of various situations involving, among other things, the projection of images and the transmission of pre-recorded music and voices through loudspeakers situated at different points around the theatre. The composer himself preferred to use the term *azione scenica* to describe the work, but this did not stop the first performance from being disturbed by members of the audience (allegedly neo-fascists) accusing Nono of betraying the tradition of Italian opera.[1]

From 1960 onwards Nono made an increasing use of material pre-recorded on magnetic tape. His first purely electronic work, *Omaggio a Emilio Vedova* (1960), could perhaps be described as an 'impression in sound' inspired by the work of the Venetian artist mentioned in the title. He soon discovered that new technology made it possible for him to extend his research into the subtle mutations of individual sounds while at the same time continuing his political and social campaign. His protests against the effect of mass industrialisation on modern humanity were particularly explicit in works like *La fabbrica illuminata* (1964), where a soprano sings live against a magnetic tape containing sounds originating from the shop-floor of a factory. A few

---

1 It is significant that from the late 1950s onwards critics, music historians and composers began to abandon the label 'opera' in favour of the more generic 'teatro musicale'. The term can safely be used to describe the multiplicity of new forms emerging during the post-war period (with or without a clearcut plot or action) and at the same time avoids the conventional connotations of the more traditional word.

years later he wrote *Non Consumiamo Marx* (1969), whose second part incorporates slogans recorded during the student protests in Paris in May 1969.

All these themes were again taken up and further expanded in his ambitious second theatrical work *Al gran sole carico d'amore* (1974), a work involving huge resources including a large chorus, special stage effects and ample use of the latest electronic and technological devices. Like *Intolleranza* the piece consists of a collage of scenes and texts written by various politically motivated authors, but here there is no definite storyline. The action passes rapidly from one historical moment to another and the only the only unifying element is the underlying social-political message itself, a cry for freedom from oppression rooted in class or race.

Al gran sole carico d'amore probably marks the culminating point in Nono's determination to use music to convey his socialist ideals. From the late 1970s onwards his approach became considerably more introspective. A more abstract exploration of the potentials of rudimentary sound can be heard in works like the *Fragmente-Sille, an Diotima* for string quartet (1980) where the use of microintervals fulfil, after more than half a century, the revolutionary dreams of Busoni. And the work also contains an unexpected tribute to Verdi, since it is largely based on the multi-intervalled 'enigmatic scale' used by the 19th century composer in his *Ave Maria* (1889), the first of the *Quattro Pezzi Sacri*. The experiments with microintervals continue in one of Nono's last full-scale orchestral works, *A Carlo Scarpa architetto* (1984), written in memory of the illustrious Venetian architect. As in *Fragmente-Stille* moments of silence and long pauses take on an increasingly important role and the extreme simplicity of the piece, which is essentially based on two alternating notes, is a far cry from the complex serialism of his earlier works.

Nono, like much of the Italian avant-garde, was a regular visitor to the recently established electronic studios in Milan (see below), but during the last decade of his life in particular he carried out much of his work outside of Italy in the German studios of the *Sudwestfunk* at Freiburg im Breisgau where he was able to take advantage of the most sophisticated technology existing at the time. Yet despite the vast resources available to him in Germany the electronic or electro-acoustic works of his last years are actually characterized by a rarefaction of sound that at times becomes almost minimalist. The soft tones of the bass flute and bass clarinet are, for example, used to extraordinary effect in *A Pierre, dell'azzurro silenzio, inquietum* (1985) and once again, as the title suggests, silence has become a fundamental element of the composition.

It was during this period of introspection and refined electro-acoustic research that Nono composed his third and final work for theatre. *Prometeo* (1984) is, to all extents and purposes, an anti-opera. Action and scenery are completely dispensed with and the two leading 'characters' are the sound and the listeners. The work was first performed in the deconsecrated church of San Lorenzo during the *Biennale di Venezia* of 1984 and marked the end of almost 15 years of altercation between the composer and the organisers of the festival.

Notwithstanding this long period of friction there is little doubt that Venice had a decisive influence on Nono's life and work. His life-long exploration of 'sound in space' can surely be traced back to the 16th century tradition of St Mark's, where ever since the Renaissance it had been common practice to set two choirs and instrumental groups at opposite sides of the church to give a spatial dimension to the music, as well as to make the most of the fascinating effects offered by the unique acoustics of the building. And it should not be forgotten that Nono's two most important teachers were both Venetians: first Malipiero, who undoubtedly did much to pass on his interest in early Italian music, and then Maderna, who played a vital part in Nono's career both as a teacher and close friend.

Although Bruno Maderna (1920-73) was born a few years before Nono and died almost twenty years earlier, his outlook, musical or otherwise, appears to have been considerably broader than that of his pupil and friend. In the end, Nono's political zeal, no matter how noble in origin, may actually have acted as a self-limiting factor in his creativity. Maderna's experiments with electronic music were, for example, more adventurous and his style as a whole was notably more eclectic, often incorporating elements of folk music and jazz. And while breaking new ground with his post-Webernian compositions, he was at the same time writing film-scores for well known Italian directors.

Like the majority of Italian composers of his time Maderna's formative years were steeped in ancient music and neo-classicism. His brief period of study with Malipiero in the 1940s enabled him to absorb his teacher's passion for the Renaissance and throughout his career he wrote many transcriptions of works by Monteverdi, G. Gabrieli and other great Italian masters. It was during the same period that he, like Nono, came into contact with Scherchen and under his guidance not only perfected his conducting technique, but also joined the German conductor in his campaign for the promotion of new music. Many of the so-called 'historical' recordings of modern Italian music dating from this period are, in fact, conducted by Maderna.

It was, however, his long association with Darmstadt that from 1949 onwards was to have the most significant and lasting influence on his musical development. So precious was the experience that after becoming a regular teacher and conductor on the Darmstadt courses, he soon chose to take up residence in the town and eventually died there. The evolution of his style during the '50s in a certain way followed the typical course taken by many other members of the group. His early neo-classicism soon gave way to an approach that at first embraced the traditional precepts of serialism but quickly developed into a much more personal approach to the system. Among other things he became fascinated with the possibilities offered by magic squares, a system of arranging numbers in a square from which short series can be derived and then applied to the pitch, duration or other aspects of a composition according to the requirements of the composer. Maderna had already toyed with this technique in several works written in the early '50s, for example in the *Quattro Lettere* for soprano, bass and chamber orchestra (1953).

During this crucial period of development Maderna also ventured into a new domain that would soon give rise to one of his greatest achievements. In 1955 he co-founded (with Berio) an electronic

Bruno Maderna

workshop in Italy that was to rival similar establishments in Europe, in particular Stockhausen's *Westdeutscher Rundfunk* and Pierre Schaeffer's RTF studio in Paris which between them had dominated the international electronic scene until then. The *Studio di Fonologia della RAI* in Milan was destined to become the focal point of electronic experimentation in Italy and until its closure in 1983 attracted a great number of the most talented Italian composers of the time.

In addition to writing purely electronic pieces (e.g. Notturno, 1956), Maderna frequently chose to base his electronic compositions on sounds derived from more traditional sources such as standard musical instruments or the voice. He was, in fact, one of the first composers to combine live instrumental music with recorded electronic music and as early as 1952 he had written the first version of his *Musica su Due Dimensioni* for flute, magnetic tape and cymbal.

A relatively new genre that emerged from the experiments carried out in the Milan studios was the 'Radiodramma' or 'Invenzione radiofonica' that took advantage of the huge popularity of the radio in those years. The possibilities offered by this very special means of communication continued to inspire Maderna right up to his very last years. One of his most successful pieces for radio was *Ages* (1972), a work where the recorded voices of children and adults reciting snatches of Shakespeare's 'All the world's a stage' (from 'As you like it') are ingeniously re-elaborated to produce what is probably Maderna's most accessible electronic composition. The following year saw the production of the more complex drama *Satyricon* (1973), an entertaining piece inspired by the work of the Latin writer Petronius.

We have already noted how the music of Luigi Nono is haunted by an underlying sense of lyricism, something he may have inherited from the Viennese serialists or more probably from the long Italian tradition of lyric opera. In the case of Maderna such lyricism is so pervading that it often becomes one of the most representative, and sometimes dominant, features of his style. Surprisingly for a member of the experimental avant-garde it is melody that plays a vital unifying role in much of his work, a task that is more often than not assigned to the woodwind and in particular to the flute and oboe. Examples of this abound in the whole of the composer's output: the opening flute solo of the *Serenata* (1954), the short *Honeyreves* for flute and piano[1], the central role of the flute in the radio play *Don Perlimplin* (1962) and in the cycle *Hyperion* (1964-66), the three oboe concertos written between 1962 and 1973, the exchange of melodic fragments between various woodwind instruments in the central part of the *Serenata per un Satellite* (1969), the *Grande Aulodia* for flute, oboe and orchestra (1970) and the rich woodwind solos in Ages, and so on.

In a radio interview recorded in 1999 Maderna's friend and fellow composer Donatoni made an interesting point about his last works. He believed that Maderna had reached his creative peak in 1969 with the composition of *Quadrivium*, an ambitious piece for four percussionists and four different instrumental groups, and from that point on had become lost in his obsessive search for novelty. Donatoni may

---

1 / The work was dedicated to the flautist Severino Gazzelloni (1919-92) who frequently took part in performances of Maderna's music — his first name has been inverted to form the unusual title of the piece.

Franco Donatoni

well have been thinking of the excesses of a later work like *Satyricon* which incorporates a bewildering array of different genres – pastiche, jazz and even the march from Verdi's Aida. A similar situation characterises the *Venetian Journal* (1971-72), which is so full of musical and stylistic references that it becomes difficult to trace the real Maderna. But as we shall see later, this was just the beginning of a trend that with the passing of time would become increasingly popular among younger composers in their attempt to reconcile the present in terms of the past and in so doing escape from the impasse that many believed to be imminent.

Donatoni was probably right in suggesting that, of the series of large-scale orchestral works written by Maderna in his last years, *Quadrivirium* is the most accomplished. The piece also offers, among other things, a fine example of the composer's very personal, non-dogmatic approach to the introduction of aleatory elements in music. Elements of chance, or rather of choice, had already appeared in other works written by Maderna in the sixties, notably in the previously mentioned *Serenata per un Satellite*, where the performers are simply given a single sheet of paper containing a series of notes to be combined at will.

Despite his retrospective criticism there is no doubt that Franco Donatoni (1927-2000) owed much to his close association with Maderna and was particularly moved by his friend's untimely demise. Their meeting at Darmstadt in the mid-fifties was to have a greater influence on Donatoni's musical development than any of his previous studies under such eminent teachers as Pizzetti and Liviabella. Shortly after Maderna's death he paid his respects with the composition of the *Duo Pour Bruno* (1974-75), which has become one of Donatoni's most regularly performed works and is fairly representative of his mature style with its solid walls of sound and relentless driving energy.

After starting his career as an admirer and emulator of Bartok, Donatoni was quickly 'converted' to serialism during his Darmstadt years and later followed the path taken by Boulez and Stockhausen in the direction of total serialism. A complex work like the *Puppenspiel I* (1961) offers the listener very little respite and although the flute has a central part in the work there is no hint of the lyricism that helped dilute the harshness of similar works by many of his Italian contemporaries.

What he did share with numerous other composers, though, was an increasing interest in the use of improvisation and indeterminacy. Elements of free choice can already be found in *For Grilly* (1960) and this was soon followed by a full adherence to the extremes proposed by John Cage, eventually leading to the adoption of alternative forms of notation. In his Fourth Quartet "Zrcadlo" (1963) the performers are simply instructed to react (musically) to headlines taken from the newspapers of the day and as such virtually take over the piece in terms of its contents and structure. The physical presence of the performers or the conductor thus became an integral part of the composition. And physical gestures take on a central role in a piece simply called *Per Orchestra* (1962), where at a certain point the conductor is instructed to direct the orchestra using signals more normally associated with a policeman guiding the rush-hour traffic!

Two aspects make Donatoni rather atypical of his time. In the first place his involvement in the fashionable field of electronic music was minimal and the only significant piece using electronics is his *Quartetto III* for magnetic tape (1961), written at a time when nearly all composers were busy sampling the exciting new possibilities offered by the medium, sometimes merely out of curiosity. Secondly, and to some extent more surprisingly, he does not appear to have been very attracted to the voice as a means to express his musical thoughts. This may seem strange for a composer coming from a recent tradition (that of his teacher Pizzetti, for instance) where vocal music was so fundamental and where the revival of Renaissance choral polyphony had been hailed by many as the way ahead. After writing very little for the voice in the 1950s he wrote nothing during the '60s and in the handful of minor pieces he composed during the late '70s the style of writing tends to be more instrumental than vocal.

It was not until the 1980s that Donatoni began to show any real interest in the expressive potentials of the voice. He even wrote an opera, *Atem* (1985), although the term 'anti-opera' might be more appropriate, given that the work contains very little scenic action. Ten years later, when his career was already reaching its close, he wrote what could be considered his only true piece of musical theatre, *Alfred, Alfred* (1995). This opéra comique, on a libretto written by the composer himself, is typically challenging for the performers – near the end of the work one of the sopranos is expected to reach a top G. But as the label suggests, the work is basically intended to be comic and is not without its humorous vein. The opera is littered, for example, with unexpected quotations or references to the works of other

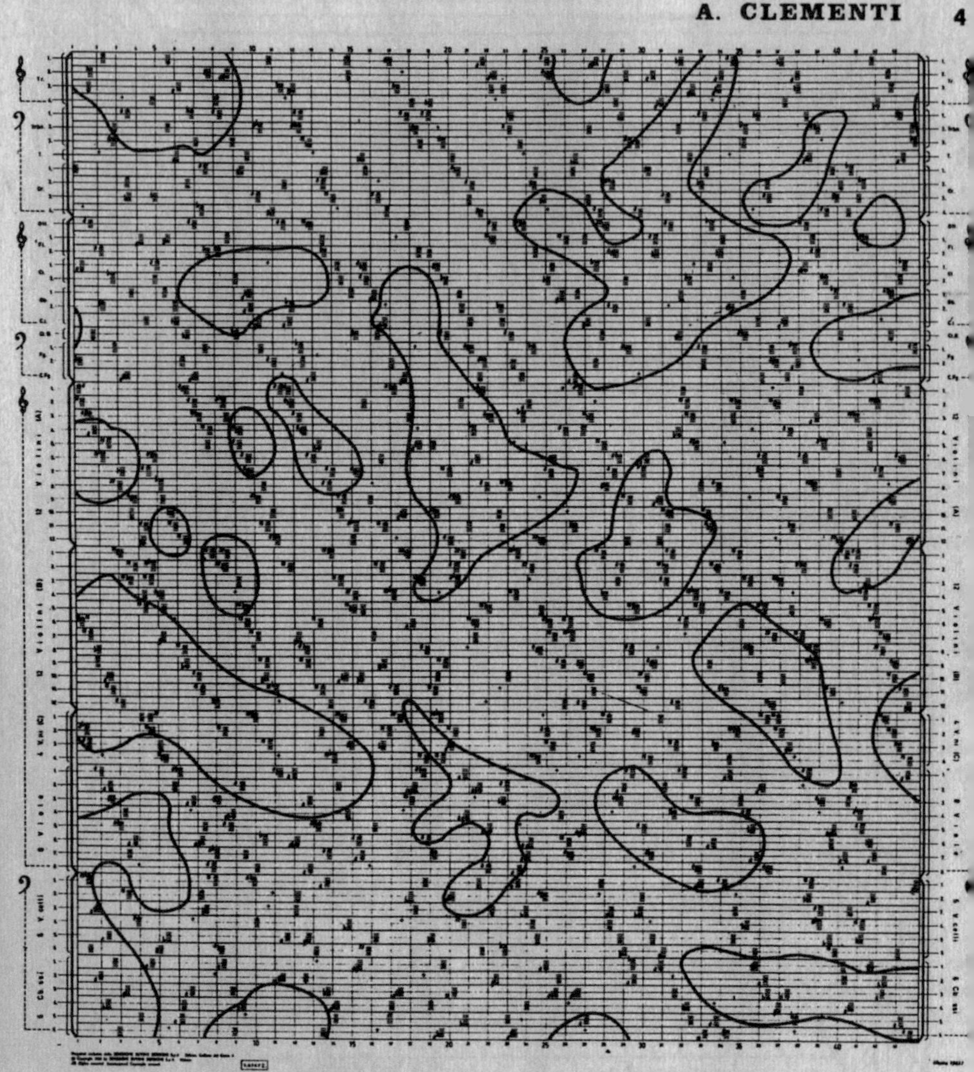

Clementi's *Informel 3*

composers (including Wagner, Stravinsky, Vivaldi, Respighi and, of course, Verdi, with particular reference to *La Traviata*). And a remarkable hint of self-irony creeps into the work when in the penultimate scene the mezzo-soprano states that she finds contemporary music incomprehensible and that even Wagner and Verdi are beyond her understanding – and at this very point she begins to sing in a lyrical style strangely reminiscent of Bellini.

There is no doubt that Donatoni's music is frequently difficult not only for the performers but also for the public at large. Typically of this somewhat introspective era his approach to composition was guided by an extreme form of rationality. Like Maderna he was extremely fascinated with numbers and the different ways they might be combined to provide the basis for a musical structure. The form of his string quartet *The Heart's Eye* (1979/80), for example, evolves geometrically both backwards and forwards from two central bars, while the number 2 plays a vital role in the construction of almost every parameter of the composition (including the metronome markings).

A further barrier for the listener is the extreme fragmentation that characterises most of Donatoni's mature output, an aspect that is often so violent that any search for linear development will inevitably be in vain. His approach to composition has even been described as a sort of 'decomposition', a very apt term to express the brutal disintegration of Wagner's music at the beginning of *Puppenspiel I*. And while it is true that the textures of some of his later compositions tend to be a little more rarefied than his earlier works – and in some cases, as in the choral piece *Madrigale* (1991), even offer a hint of tonality – his music nevertheless remains hard for many to digest.

Equally complex is the music of Aldo Clementi (1925-), a pupil of Sangiorgi[1] and Petrassi who from 1955-62 followed the Darmstadt courses. The complexity of his mature style differs from that of Donatoni in that it is not the result of obsessive fragmentation but rather of unrelenting continuity. Part of Clementi's philosophy regarded detail as unimportant and the whole as an end in itself. After passing from neo-classicism to total serialism he subsequently embarked on a totally new direction with the composition of the chamber works *Informel* 1-3 (1961-63). From then on his music became intensely contrapuntal, forming a mosaic of continuously revolving sounds that often finishes as abruptly as it began. The counterpoint may at times involve an impressive number of parts. In the *Concerto* for wind

---

1 Alfredo Sangiorgi (1894-1962), who had studied with Schoenberg in Vienna.

and 2 pianos (1967) there are no less than 48 separate parts, but this is nothing compared to the 144 parts of the *Variante A* for choir and orchestra (1964) and the extraordinary 500 different lines in the *Passacaglia per flauto e nastro magnetico* (first performed 1989) which was so complicated that several years had to pass before new technology could provide a means for its performance.

Many Italian composers who had taken part in the Darmstadt courses subsequently felt the need to continue the diffusion of the so-called *Neue Musik* in their own country. The most significant step taken in this direction was the founding of *Nuova Consonanza* in 1960, an association set up in Rome with the specific aim of performing and promoting contemporary music. However, as the name suggests (literally 'New Consonance'), the association's intention was not simply to transfer the Darmstadt experience into an Italian context, but rather to embrace a much wider range of innovative styles and techniques. Four years later, in 1964, the *Gruppo di Improvvisazione Nuova Consonanza* emerged from within the association, a startlingly original undertaking made all the more unique by the fact that all its members were both composers and performers, thus eliminating the gap that had till then existed between creator and interpreter.

One of founder members of *Nuova Consonanza* and of the *Gruppo di Improvvisazione* was Franco Evangelisti (1926-80), a composer who had attended the Darmstadt courses during the 1950s and, in particular, had spent several years studying with Stockhausen. His fervent search for totally new means of expression led him first of all to dissociate himself from any musical school or current and eventually to abandon composition altogether on account of his apparent failure to achieve his very demanding personal goals.[1] His most important output dates from the end of the '50s and beginning of the '60s and

---

1 A fascinating parallel can be seen here between Evangelisti's thoughts and those of the Futurists. The crisis which had arisen at the turn of the century regarding the redundancy of most traditional forms and formulas led the exponents of Futurism to advocate a much freer approach to their artistic expression, an approach that often implied the use of choice and chance. As we have seen, though, their efforts had little or no influence on their immediate successors (see Chapter 2)

includes *Aleatorio* for string quartet (1959) and *Random or not Random* for orchestra (1962), works, as their names suggest, involving a large element of choice on the part of the performer. He dedicated the rest of his short life first and foremost to reflection and continued his experiments in electronic music at a more intimate level, teaching his findings to his students in Rome.

A slightly younger composer who became active in the work of the group just a few years after its birth was Francesco Pennisi (1934-2000). As was the case with many of those involved it was not so much a question of musical style that united them but more a common passion for the new. Although he made very little use of electronics, he enthusiastically took up other innovative aspects such as graphic notation and the inclusion of visual elements in a performance, something that came quite naturally to him as a talented amateur painter. His one-act 'scena' *Silvia Simplex* (1972) is accompanied by the projection of a series of his own drawings illustrating the topic of this 'musical talk' (i.e. the wonders of flight). And a prepared or partially prepared piano plays a central part in works like *Serena* (1973) and later still in *La muse endormie* (1981).

Other founder members of *Nuova Consonanza* included Domenico Guaccero (1927-84) and Egisto Macchi (1928-92), both of whom wrote works making use of the most advanced procedures available at the time, but whose music is now seldom heard. Their importance lies rather in their contribution to the promotion of experimental music through their administrative and teaching posts at various institutions and festivals. With the help and enthusiasm of the original members and subsequently of younger musicians and composers the work of the group soon became an established part of the contemporary scene both in Italy and abroad, and its important role in the divulgence of new music appears set to continue well into the future.

The somewhat exceptional case of the involvement of a composer who was actually older than the founding members of the group was that of Giancinto Scelsi (1905-1988). This fact can be partly explained by the extraordinary modernity of the music he wrote from the '50s onwards, a modernity that to a large extent paralleled (or perhaps even rivalled) what was being developed in Darmstadt.

Scelsi's role in *Nuova Consonanza* was in reality quite marginal. His original approach to composition and his reclusive tendencies made it difficult for him to belong to any school or movement. After a period of adherence to serialism, a direction he had taken after a stay in Vienna during the 1930s, he soon developed a freer, much more individual style. From the 1950s onwards he was strongly influenced by oriental mysticism and thought, and such titles as the *Quattro illustrazioni sulla Metamorfosi di Visnù* for piano (1953) or *Krishna e Rada* for flute and piano (1986) leave little doubt as to their inspiration. He eventually reached a point where he refused the label of 'composer', preferring to be called a 'postino', that is, a sort of messenger conveying his mystic inspiration into the material world.

His almost obsessive research into the potentials of single repeated sounds led him to experiment with microintervals as a means of varying individual notes without moving too far away from the basic pitch. This technique is especially suited to the characteristics of stringed instruments and is widely exploited in his fourth quartet (1964), where each string of each instrument is given its own stave in order to resolve the difficulties in notation. But despite the apparent complexity of his writing the resulting soundscapes are marked by an overwhelming simplicity that doubtlessly has its roots in oriental and Buddhist philosophy. In each of the *Quattro pezzi per orchestra da camera (su una nota sola)* (1959) the music is reduced to a single basic note that undergoes variations in dynamics and texture, while any mutations in pitch amount to little more than a few microintervals. Even in much larger-scale compositions like *Uaxuctum* (1966) the music is powerful yet remarkably uncluttered. And when listening to the awesome swells of sound that exploit the very lowest registers of the orchestra it is hard not to hear echoes of the Tibetan mountain horn or of the deep, longdrawn growls of Tibetan monks.

A certain controversy nevertheless surrounds the works of Scelsi. The fact that he came from an extremely wealthy family (his full name was Count Gacinto Scelsi d'Ayala Valva) meant that he was able to meet all the expenses for the publication and promotion of his music. However, shortly after the composer's death a dispute arose as to how much of his work was genuinely his own. The otherwise conservative composer Vieri Tosatti (see Chapter 5) had worked in close association with Scelsi and in an article entitled 'Giancinto Scelsi c'est moi' (Il Giornale della Musica, January 1989) he claimed the credit for much of the music written during their 30 years of collaboration.

Yet even if Tosatti's claims were true, the outcome would not detract from the composer's basic philosophy: the inspiration was the fundamental element of any composition, the material side of the work (including the actual writing of the score) being to all extents and purposes of secondary interest.

Like many other Italian composers of the 20th century Scelsi has been appreciated first and foremost abroad, above all in Germany and in France. The French experimental group Itinéraire did much to promote his music during the 1970s and his style was to have a considerable influence on the composers of so-called 'spectral music'[1]. It was not until after his death that his genius and originality began to attract attention also in Italy and his importance was finally given full recognition in 2003 when a number of recordings and documents were collected in the Archivio di Musica Contemporanea in Bologna. However, the greater part of the work of this visionary composer remains firmly under lock and key in his family home in Rome.

---

[1] A group of French composers, notably Murail, Grisey and Levinas, who were fascinated by the possibilities offered by the natural spectrum of a sound, often resulting in the use of micro-intervals. The movement was particularly active in Paris during the 1970s, most of the members having previously studied there with Messiaen.

7

THE GOOD, THE BAD AND THE POPULAR

For many Italians the USA represented freedom, democracy and above all modernity. When the U.S. troops finally embarked in Salerno in September 1943 they brought with them not only hopes of a better future, but also American cigarettes, chocolate, chewing gum and, more to the point, the dance music of Glen Miller.

Popular (as opposed to folk) music was by no means a new concept to the Italians. We have already seen how in the early years of the 20th century the *canzonetta* had enjoyed an unprecedented success at the hands of composers such as Tosti and Denza (see Chapter 1). However, from the 1920s onwards a whole new genre of song had virtually been imposed on the nation. Lyrics that basically amounted to fascist propaganda were set to 'catchy' tunes and could be heard everywhere – not only on the radio, but also in bars and tea-rooms.[1] This new style of popular music thus became a type of musical Big Brother, following citizens from their homes to the squares and back home again. And since the playing and broadcasting of foreign music, and in particular jazz, was strictly controlled and therefore rarely heard there was very little room for any alternative, at least as far as the general population was concerned.

---

1 One of the most notorious of the fascist songs was *Faccetta nera* ('Little black face') which spoke of the wonderful new life that awaited those moving (or forced to move) to the Italian colonies in East Africa. The song was eventually banned in 1937 on account of its reference to a taboo relationship between an Italian soldier and an African girl.

Sanremo sheet music cover

The situation among the bourgeoisie was a little different in that they obviously had more extensive means and thus greater access to the outside world. Mussolini himself is said to have been very fond of Laurel and Hardy movies and one of his sons, Romano, actually became a professional jazz pianist. And the fact that Italian jazz groups were allowed to continue their activity throughout the 1930s, albeit in a limited way, and that even the American Louis Armstrong was conceded two concerts in Turin in 1935, is surely clear enough evidence that exposure to the genre was not so restricted as is sometimes reported.

When all barriers had finally been removed it took less than a decade for the influx of American culture and fashion to reach flood-like proportions. The success of Glen Miller was soon surpassed by the arrival on the scene of Frank Sinatra and Dean Martin, both of whom were all the more venerated on account of their Italian origins. As the sixties progressed it became increasingly common to hear so-called 'cover' versions of American (and sometimes British) pop songs that had been translated and then re-recorded by the growing number of Italian groups or soloists – ironically many people were not immediately aware of the American/British originals and were often convinced that these songs represented a new wave of popular Italian culture[1].

But despite this foreign invasion the much-loved Italian melody still found its place and was epitomised in the San Remo Festival of popular Italian song, established in the 1950s and subsequently an annual event that continued to be popular far into the following century. The Festival, which concentrates on sentimental ballads and more recently on soft rock, could easily be dismissed as trite, yet its appeal, at least in its earliest years, was truly international and certain songs presented at the competition achieved world fame. Domenico Modugno's *Volare* (*Nel blu dipinto di blu*) was, and still is, one of the greatest Italian ex-

---

1 A classic example of this is Procol Harem's *A Whiter Shade of Pale* which in Italian became Senza Luce and was a big hit for the group I Dik Dik. There was even a translated version of *White Christmas* (*Bianca Natale*) which for years deprived the Italian public of Bing Crosby's classic crooning.

ports of all time.

The period also saw a brief but highly successful spate of Italian musicals which, despite being clearly modelled on their American counterpart, were exquisitely Italian in their subject-matter and melodic style. Undoubtedly the most celebrated writers/directors of this genre were Pietro Garinei (1919-2006) and Sandro Giovannini (1915-1977), whose biggest hits include *Rugantino* (1962) and *Aggiungi un posto a Tavola* (1974), both written in collaboration with the composer Armondo Trovaioli (1917-).

A more weighty branch of popular music was epitomized by the cantautore, a special brand of singer/songwriter, whose lyrics usually contained a message, more often than not of a political nature. Many of the most committed artists worked for the record label Del Sole, an overtly leftwing enterprise that specialized in protest songs. Singers like Giovanna Marini (1937-) had a huge following during the years of student unrest, although much of her output was forgotten when the revolutionary spirit had been quelled. She remains famous as a collector and performer of traditional and semi-traditional folksongs such as *Bella Ciao*, a song, incidentally, that took on new life (with new words) in the hands of the Italian resistance who used it to counteract the jingoistic fascist hymns.[1]

Slowly but surely the influence of popular music or *musica leggera* (light music) began to have a marked influence on what the Italians like to call *musica colta* (literally 'cultured music'). We have already seen how composers like Bruno Maderna had already begun to incorporate elements of jazz into works like *Don Perlimplin* in the early '60s. Another outstanding example of how this new genre was assimilated into Italian culture can be found in the music of Giorgio Gaslini (1927-). Not only was he one of the first musicians ever to propose jazz courses at an Italian conservatory, but he even went as far as to invent a form of 'serial jazz' (e.g. in his *Dall'alba all'alba*, 1964) where the rules of serialism were applied to a composition written in a jazz idiom. And it was largely thanks to Gaslini that talented Italian jazz

---

1 Giovanna Marini is the daughter of the early twentieth century composer Giovanni Salviucci (see Chapter 2)

musicians such as Gianluigi Trovesi (1944-) were able to establish themselves on the national and international scene.

Luciano Berio (1925-2003), too, embraced popular culture as an essential element of his highly eclectic font of inspiration. His *Laborintus II* (1965), for example, features a wide range of references including jazz and street cries, the latter theme being developed more explicitly some years later in his *Cries of London* (1974-75).

The flexibility required by jazz singers and they way they played with individual words and sounds was much admired by Berio, whose tireless exploration of the human voice was to become a hallmark of his output throughout the '60s and '70s. He often showed a genuine interest not only in words as a source of sound to be manipulated, but also in the actual language to which they belonged. It is not unusual to find a combination of several different languages within a single piece. In *Laborintus II*, which was originally commissioned by the French radio to celebrate the 700th anniversary of the birth of Dante, the Italian text by Edoardo Sanguineti is supplemented by snatches of poetry by T.S Eliot and Ezra Pound. In the monumental *Sinfonia for 8 voices and orchestra* (1968-69) we hear not only lines taken from Samuel Beckett (in English), but also the occasional interjection in French and German. The work could be said to epitomise Berio's fascination with every kind of musical language, for it is made up of a myriad of musical quotations taken from the most famous works of the 19th and 20th century that are so skilfully sewn together that it is virtually impossible to notice the 'joins'.

Berio found further inspiration in the extraordinarily versatile voice of his American wife Cathy Berberian. In what is probably the best known piece from the series, the *Sequenza III* (1966) is a landmark composition that explores all aspects of vocality, including singing, speaking, whispering and shouting. Berio had already taken advantage of his wife's unique vocal skills in his electronic masterpiece *Thema (Omaggio a Joyce)* (1958) produced at the newly established *Studio di Fonologia della RAI* in Milan (see Chapter 6). The piece focuses above all on individual vowels and consonants, transforming them into a vast array of fantastic, yet meaningful sounds.

Luciano Berio

For a composer so fascinated by language and the human voice it is not surprising that Berio was particularly attracted to the theatre. Yet the number of works that could actually be labelled as 'operas' (in the broadest sense of the term, given their highly experimental form and content) is fairly limited. This category might include *Opera* (1969-70) and two works based on texts by Italo Calvino, *La Vera Storia* (1976-79) and *Un re in ascolto* (1982-83). Later works such as

Outis (1996) and *La Cronaca del luogo* (1999) are perhaps better defined as 'anti-operas' in that they go out of their way to avoid any form of dramatic narration. *Outis* in particular returns to the concept of *teatro a pannelli* originally experimented with by Malipiero (see Chapter 3). The work (which Berio describes as an *azione musicale*) is loosely based on the epic tale of Ulysses – something of a recurring theme among composers of the second half of the 20th century. But to search for any dramatic development, or even a satisfactory ending would be somewhat in vain. Berio focuses instead on the solitude surrounding characters like Penelope and tries to draw analogies with the lack of communication that he believed intrinsic to modern society.

In reality a large proportion of his 'non-operatic' works (including the previously mentioned *Laborintus II*) can be justifiably described as theatrical, since they are often intended for the stage and generally involve several actors/speakers. Even many of Berio's smaller-scale solo pieces call for a visual/gestural element that turns the musical performance into more of a 'spectacle'. While performing the *Sequenza V* (1966) the solo trombonist is required to be partly dressed as a clown and is instructed to go through a series of movements/gestures during the course of the piece, some of which are specifically marked on the score while others are left up to the interpretation of the performer.

Over and above his undoubted creative genius Berio was also a skilled musical technician. Apart from his 'rewriting' of works by Schubert and Brahms in the 1980s, his most daring venture came in the first years of the new millennium when he completed an alternative ending to Puccini's *Turandot*. This new, less dramatic rendering of the third act was met with great critical acclaim at its first performance in Los Angeles (25 May 2002), but whether or not it manages to usurp Alfano's classic version remains to be seen.

Berio's greatness also lies in the fact that throughout his long and fruitful career he steadfastly stuck to his own individual creative path irrespective of the trends and fashions of the moment. It is surely significant that his *Piano Sonata*, written at the very beginning of the new millennium, gave little space to the growing trend among many younger composers to write simpler, more directly communicative music. The sheer complexity of the Sonata shows that despite the many changes that had taken place in Italian society during the last 40 years of the century, Berio still firmly believed in the fundamental right of the creative artist to think for himself and not to bow to the pressure of conformity. Elements of simplicity and humour are, of course, frequently encountered in his music, but they are never allowed to stand in the way of substance.

On the other hand, he could not be accused of taking on the die-hard attitude adopted by many of his fellow composers, especially those who had taken serialism to its extremes in the 1950s and adamantly refused to make their music more appetising for the general public. The breach between the two factions – the committed followers of Webern on the one hand and the more liberal individualists on the other – reached such a point that it even became customary in certain intellectual circles to divide contemporary composers into two categories: the *buoni* and the *cattivi* (basically, the 'good and the bad guys').

Exactly how a composer was classed as *buono* or *cattivo* is not altogether clear. There would seem to be some connection with the 'vows' taken during the early years of the Darmstadt school. Those who remained faithful to the hard line adopted in favour of serialism seem to have been considered more 'serious' and certainly more provocative than those who had subsequently gone their own way. The origins of this division can also be traced back to the thoughts and writings of the German musicologist Adorno (1903-69), whose theories were extremely influential in central Europe and consequently among the Italian avant-garde. Adorno's most significant accusation was levelled against the twentieth century neo-classical movement, whose adherents he saw as being bourgeois and decadent. The only true path to modern music was, according to him, the one pursued by the New Viennese school under the guidance of Schoenberg and his successors.

The extent to which many Italian composers and critics took this particular brand of essentially left-wing philosophy to heart may at

first seem a little excessive. It should not be forgotten, though, that
the 1960s and '70s saw a great deal of political unrest characterised
by frequent industrial action and student protests. On top of this
many intellectuals and musicians active in the post-war period were
inevitably caught up in a backlash of anti-Fascism, and their interpretation of the theories of Adorno therefore tended to go hand in
hand with their socialist ideals. From this point of view, music had
now become well and truly mixed up with politics, even though it
should be underlined that the majority of such socially motivated
composers tended to opt for a slightly more subtle approach than
the one adopted by Nono (see Chapter 6).

Generally speaking, the social commitment of composers like Armando Gentilucci (1939-89), one of the most important pupils of
Donatoni, becomes manifest mostly through his choice of texts: the
Canti di Majakowskij (1970) was, for example, based on poems by the
Soviet poet who gave the work its name. The same could be said of
Giacomo Manzoni (1932-), who like Gentilucci had studied at the
then prolific and forward-looking Milan Conservatory. Although he
chose to dedicate much of his time to the translation of the writings
of Adorno and also wrote an authoritative book on Schoenberg, the
expression of his strong political views were again reflected more in
the socio-political themes that often underlie his works rather than
in any dramatic confrontation.

Manzoni's first opera, *La Sentenza* (1960) combines an overtly political issue with a musical language that reveals a more or less rigid
application of total serialism. However, in his second opera *Atomtod*
(1965), inspired by the fears of the anti-nuclear movement of those
years, and again in *Ombre* for orchestra and choir (1968), dedicated
to the memory of Che Guevara, there is already evidence of a much
broader spectrum of musical inspiration. Apart from the topicality
of the subject matter itself, the two works also display many features
fashionable among the avant-garde: the use of electronics, the introduction of some aleatory elements and the occasional reference to
jazz and popular music.

As his style developed he became increasingly fascinated with the rich textures resulting from the use of polyrhythms and tone clusters, the latter reflecting his great admiration for Edgar Varèse, to whom he dedicated his *Masse* for piano and orchestra (1977). The much loved 'sound masses' cultivated by Varèse and his followers feature prominently in many of Manzoni's later works, especially those involving choral ensembles, where the nature of the instrument (i.e. the voice) lends itself perfectly to the desired effect.

Interestingly, the development of Manzoni's style also offers us a clear insight into the evolution of electronic techniques during the last decades of the century: from the use of pre-recorded material on magnetic tape in *Parole da Beckett* (1970-71) to the free and sophisticated combination of recorded material and live electronics in late works such as *Quanto oscura selva trovai* (1995).

Two other composers who were initially caught up in the wave of total serialism but then happily went along their own way were Sylvano Bussotti (1931-) and Niccolò Castiglioni (1932-1996). Both had some contact with Darmstadt but neither of them were really convinced that the strict adhesion to Webernian thought advocated by the likes of Boulez was able to offer a long-term solution to the needs of the modern composer. They were, in fact, among the first of many Italian composers who did not reject serialism as such, but preferred to temper it with a more directly communicative approach that in many cases involved a partial return to tonality.

Bussotti represents a fascinating example of an esteemed and often quoted composer whose music is nevertheless seldom heard. After touching on the extremes of experimentation in the early '60s under the influence of John Cage he eventually turned to a more colourful, sometimes eccentric manner. Apart from large-scale orchestral works like the *Semi di Gramsci* (1967-70) for string quartet and orchestra, a stunning piece and probably his most frequently performed work, Bussotti channelled most of his creative energy into writing for the theatre in its widest sense.

From the '70s onwards he became increasingly interested in exploring everything the theatre could possibly offer. Building on the experience of earlier works like *La Passion selon Sade* (1966), where he had given free rein to his belief in freedom of sensual expression, he wrote a long series of spectacular works, perhaps typified by the extravagant *Lorenzaccio* (1972), where music, dance, mime and acting are combined to produce not an opera, but something closer to the 'happenings' that were so fashionable at the time.[1]

But despite the fact that his activity as a composer has continued into the 21st century and new pieces such as the *Modello* for violin and orchestra (2000) or the semi-autobiographical *Sylvano, Sylvano* (2003) still attract the attention of the media, Bussotti is most likely to be remembered above all for the delightfully decorative graphic notation for which he first became famous. The visually elaborate scores for the *5 Piano Pieces for David Tudor* (1959) would not, in fact, look at all out of place in a gallery of modern art and he even went as far as taking his graphic scores 'on the road'. Together with his friend and like-minded composer Giuseppe Chiari (1926-), whose so-called 'action music' was deeply inspired by the music and thoughts of John cage, he eventually took his unusual exhibition on a tour that covered much of Europe and the USA.

The move away from total serialism towards a more personal (but certainly less flamboyant) idiom is again noticeable in the music of Castiglioni. After studying composition with Ghedini in Milan he subsequently went to Salzburg and then to Darmstadt, where he became absorbed in the experimental trends of the late '50s. However, after reaching the extremes of post-expressionism in works like *Eine kleine Weihnachtmusik* for chamber orchestra (1960) he began to look for an alternative path. At first this led him to make a tentative return to tonality, for instance in his *Ode* for two pianos, wind and percussion (1966), and in his *3rd Symphony* (1968-69), which he blatantly labelled as being in do (in C major). His search soon took him further afield and his sources of inspiration widened to include the music of the Middle Ages and the Renaissance, as well as an appropriation of certain oriental styles that resulted in rhythmic patterns

---

1 In the 1960s Bussotti had become well known for translating eroticism into music. In a piece entitled *Il Nudo* (1966) the soprano's melody is progressively 'stripped' of its instrumental clothing until it is left 'bare' in front of the audience.

Ennio Morricone

very close to those employed by Messiaen. Both of these elements are quite conspicuous in later works like the *Cantus Planus* (1990) and the *Liedlein* (1991-93), where his partiality for small-scale choral textures and his persistent use of the highest vocal registers produce an intricate mosaic of refreshing, almost hypnotic musical lines.

Finally, mention should be made of the continuing popularity of the cinema in Italy and the great opportunities that this now well-established art form offered to composers. Following closely in the tracks of Nino Rota (see Chapter 5) was one of the most familiar names in modern Italian music, Ennio Morricone (1928-). With the aid of the talented director Sergio Leone, Morricone was destined to achieve world-wide fame thanks to his scores for the so-called 'spaghetti westerns' (*The Good the Bad and the Ugly*, *A fistful of Dollars* etc.). Like countless other Italians before him Morricone's speciality was melody writing and he took the art to new heights when he wrote the soundtrack to Joffè's film *The Mission* (1985), which argu-ably contains some of the most memorable tunes ever written.

But there is another lesser known side to Morricone. After his early studies with Petrassi he soon turned in the direction of serialism and produced various works that make a more or less strict use of the system. In the mid-6os he even joined the avant-garde group *Nuova Consonanza* and occasionally toyed with the concept of indetermi-nacy. From the 1970s onwards, though, he gradually developed his own eclectic style that led to the composition of such accomplished works as the *Secondo concerto per flauto, violoncello e orchestra* (1985) or the *Due pezzi sacri* (1990).

Morricone remains one of the most active composers of his gen-eration, holding regular summer courses in Italy and generally maintaining a high profile. The publicity surrounding his commission to write a piece for the 2002 Ravenna Festival is perhaps symptomatic of his continuing success, while the piece itself, a choral work enti-tled *Voci dal Silenzio*, skilfully integrates live and pre-recorded music and demonstrates how he has been able to capture the essence of late twentieth century modernity without compromising his popularity. In many ways he could be said to be one of the first composers to have successfully bridged the much discussed gap between *musica colta* and *musica leggera* and at the same time distanced himself from the now obsolete divide between the *buoni* and the *cattivi*.

8

NEW VENTURES, OLD THEMES

The political unrest and terrorism that had plagued Italy during the 1970s reached its dramatic climax with the kidnapping and assassination of the prime minister Aldo Moro in 1978 and the devastating bomb attacks which targeted the Italian train network during the early 1980s. Thankfully this tragic and unnerving scenario slowly gave way to a more moderate climate and coincided with an economic recovery that brought about a sense of well-being and optimism.

It was a period of relative calm that saw the decline of the two political extremes, the Partito Comunista Italiano on the left and the Movimento Sociale Italiano on the right, both of which were divided by internal differences and eventually transformed into minority parties. In their place new moderate parties were hastily put together in a seemingly haphazard fashion, often uniting groups with a vastly different political outlook. In particular Umberto Bossi's secessionist movement the Lega Nord managed to find its way into various different governments and provocatively used the celebrated chorus *Va, pensiero* from Verdi's *Nabucco* as an anthem for their controversial cause.

Extremes also became unfashionable in the world of music. The hard line taken by socially motivated composers like Nono and Manzoni no longer seemed appropriate and the concept of the *buoni* and *cattivi*, such a burning issue in the 1970s, now seemed to have lost its relevance. Like *opera lirica* at the beginning of the 19th century, the cult of serialism, or at least total serialism, was fast becoming out of fashion and an increasing number of composers began to look for a more spontaneous means of expression.

There were, of course, those who were reluctant to give up what had been created with such fervour and commitment during the first two decades after the end of fascist rule and many still found the line established during the later years in Darmstadt a fruitful source of inspiration even after the spirit of innovation had begun to lose its initial vigour. Cage's revolutionary concept of choice and chance continued to inspire composers like Marcello Panni (1940-) well into the 1980s, while the fascination for rationalised mathematical structures can still be seen in the mature works of Alessandro Solbiati (1956-), whose *Quartetto con Lied* (1991), completely based on the ratio 1:3, would certainly have met with the approval of his teacher Donatoni.

For some composers the rupture with serialism and its various de-rivatives was abrupt and even dramatic. The Venetian conductor and composer Giuseppe Sinopoli (1946-2001) had begun to attend the Darmstadt summer courses towards the end of the '60s and then in 1970 had studied composition with Donatoni in Siena. His contact

Alessandro Solbiati

with the well-affirmed and staunchly serialist composer at first resulted in a highly complex and introspective musical language, well illustrated in the three *Tombeau d'Amour* (1975, 1976, 1977). But his style took a drastic turn some years later when he argued bitterly with his teacher about the continued use of such an unbending approach, maintaining that contemporary music was falling into a state of decadent 'mechanicalism'. The last works he wrote in the few years before taking his drastic decision to give up composition reveal a much less rigid approach. His opera *Lou Salomè* (1981), in particular, uses an idiom that waivers between late romanticism and early expressionism.

Sinopoli's decision to stop composing was accompanied by his declared resolve to prevent the performance of any of his works. He nevertheless continued his important work as a conductor and at the same time dedicated much time to writing articles and essays about music. Sinopoli is said to have declared his intention to interrupt his composing career for a period of no less than twenty years, by which time he hoped that the air would have cleared a little. Ironically, he died exactly twenty years after making this vow.

In most cases the break with serialism was much less painful. Many composers who had lived through the intense experimentation of the late 1950s and early '60s approached the 1980s with a generally more relaxed attitude. Even those who had been involved in the initial experimental phase of *Nuova Consonanza* (see Chapters 6 & 7) often returned to a more traditional idiom once the passion for the new had died down. Paolo Renosto (1935-88), once an active member of the group, moved from the extremes of *Players* (1968), where the freedom of interpretation still shows a marked influence of John Cage, to the melancholy, almost melodic language of later works like the *Valse Soirée* for chamber orchestra (1988). And a marked move away from experimentation can also be found in the later works of Azio Corghi (1937 -), who in the 1960s had been extremely active in various improvisational groups, but by the end of the '70s had turned towards a decidedly more personal idiom that incorporates different styles, techniques and resources, and moves freely between tonality and atonality according to the desired effect.

Likewise, although the lesson of his teacher Manzoni remains evident in his fondness for dense textures and lively polyrhythms, the compositions of Adriano Guarnieri (1947 -) become notably more personalised from the mid-1970s onwards, abounding in energy and often demanding a vocal virtuosity closer to that associated with jazz singers. The extraordinary agility required of the two singers in the '10 azioni liriche' *Orfeo cantando ... tolse* (1994) makes the work particularly challenging for classically trained singers and it is certainly no chance that one of his most celebrated works, the cantata *Medea* (1991), bears the dedication 'offerti a Mina' – literally 'offered to Mina', one of Italy's greatest jazz voices of all time.

As the concept of atonality became progressively outdated as a general indicator of modernity, a growing number of composers in Italy, as elsewhere, began to turn their interests towards a simpler approach where timbre, or tone colour, was often the most important element. Claudio Vacchi (1949-), for example, who studied under such eminent teachers as Manzoni and Donatoni, managed to shed his serialist inheritance and eventually developed a more eclectic style which focusses on the delicate interplay between varying layers of sound. This feature is especially prominent in what is probably his most regularly performed piece, *Dai Calanchi di Sabbiuno* (1995-97), a sort of threnody written in memory of the Italian partisans who died in the small hill town near Bologna during World War II. The version for full orchestra (it was originally written for a small chamber ensemble) is characterised by a vivid wash of contrasting tone colours where the transparent textures slowly evolve into new shapes against a regular, almost tormented pulsating beat.

A distinct emphasis on timbre can also be found in the works of two contemporary composers from Rome, Alessandro Sbordoni (1948-) and Mauro Cardi (1955-). Sbordoni's *Sull'orlo della tua memoria* (1994) explores the rich and dark tones of the bass clarinet and cello, while his more energetic but equally colourful settings of Emily Dickinson in the song-cycle *Fantasia delle Lontananza* (1992) are fast becoming a modern classic. Cardi similarly concentrates on developing the potential variations in colour offered by small chamber ensembles, as in his *Effetto Notte* (1989) where the familar tones of wind and stringed instruments are combined with the more delicate sounds of the guitar and mandolin.

The fascination with subtle shades of musical colour reaches its apotheosis in the works of Salvatore Sciarrino (1947-), one of Italy's most interesting and original contemporary composers[1]. His minute explorations of sound in its purest form have much in common with the French avant-garde working in Paris (see Chapter 6) and his contribution to the modern woodwind repertoire is nothing less than monumental. By exploiting to the full the unusual effects produced by key-clicking or special breathing techniques, he manages to conjure up intriguing new sounds from traditional instruments, despite the great deal of energy already channelled into this field over the previous four decades. His *Venere che le Grazie la fioriscano* (1989), for example, explores the musical and mechanical properties of the solo flute, continuing and expanding the revolutionary techniques first introduced some forty years before by Berio in his *Sequenza I* . Similarly, *Omaggio a Burri* (1995) focuses on the potentials of the bass flute, bass clarinet and violin, displaying an extraordinary inventiveness that places Sciarrino among the greatest modern writers for solo instruments.

Perhaps even more striking than his ability to produce new sounds from old means is Sciarrino's innovative, almost revolutionary use of silence. Although other Italians before him had increasingly explored this area (e.g. Nono in his last pieces) none of them had succeeded so well in charging the pauses with such intense emotion. In the booklet accompanying his album *Esplorazione del Bianco* (1995), which collects various pieces written in the '80s and '90s, the composer compared his use of silence with the artist Kandinsky's use of the colour white: "a silence that is not dead but full of potential". Apart from their highly rarefied use of sound, the pieces that make up the collection also illustrate how Sciarrino was not dependent on new technology or

---

1 Luigi Nono dedicated one of his very last works, *La lontananza nostalgica utopica futura* (1988-89), to Sciarrino, describing him as a "caminante esemplare" (literally, a "walking example").

electronics to achieve his objectives – natural sounds, whether strictly linked with the mechanics of a musical instrument or drawn from nature itself, have continued to be an important source of inspiration. In his *Studi per l'intonazione del Mare* (2000) he uses a veritable army of 100 flutes and 100 saxophones to recreate the whisperings of the wind and the sea. And in works like *Introduzione all'oscuro* (1981), the sound of breathing, with no electronic elaboration except amplification, plays a unifying role, virtually taking on the status of a sort of leitmotif.

The exploration of natural sounds was taken to its extreme limits by Albert Mayr (1943-), a composer from Bolzano in the mountainous north of Italy. He quite literally went 'back to nature' by scrupulously sampling and elaborating the everyday sounds that surrounded him, even going as far as attempting to capture the inaudible frequencies emanating from substances like rock Unlike Sciarrino his research necessarily involved the most advanced electronic equipment available to him. And like R. Murray Schafer before him, whose *Soundscape Studies* in the early 1970s had inspired a whole generation of 'musical ecologists', Mayr had a mission to accomplish – to try to make people more aware of the increasing levels of noise pollution that have invaded our lives in the name of progress, an interesting contrast to the point of view held by the futurist Russolo who had taken great pleasure in reproducing and subjecting his audiences to modern industrial noise.

Both Sciarrino and Mayr had, in their own way, realised that the time had come to move away from the complex and sometimes over-rationalised products of serialism. On the same basis – though in quite another direction – a fair proportion of the last generation of young composers working in the twentieth century chose to abandon the hardcore experimentation of the Darmstadt years in favour of a more simplistic, and some would say less challenging approach to music. Some have taken their cue from the so-called minimalism of Philip Glass & co. or have found their way into the world of New Age. This new 'post-modern' approach to composition, which allows the listener direct and generally unproblematic access to the intentions of the composer, has meant that many of these younger composers have reached a wider audience than many of their venerable predecessors. The genre is well suited to the expedients of the mass recording industry and it has become increasingly common for composers to release collections of pieces on albums. A case in point is Ludovico Einaudi (1955-), whose CD of piano music entitled *Le Onde* (1996) helped bring him international fame. And this trend was unequivocally confirmed in the early years of the new millenium by the massive sales achieved by the young pianist Giovanni Allevi (1969-) with his album *Joy* (2006).

A similarly uncomplicated approach has been adopted by the Sicilian composer and cellist Giovanni Sollima (1962-), whose numerous works for cello and small instrumental ensembles have attracted much attention abroad, notably in the USA, where he was hailed as the musical heir to Berio after the New York performances of his *Aquilarco* (1998). His style features long sweeping melodies often with modal or oriental inflections, lending a mystic, or perhaps meditative atmosphere to much of his work, an aspect well illustrated in what is probably his best known piece, *Spasimo* (1995).

During the last decade of the century the city of Milan became a particularly active centre for post-modernism in Italy. The writing and performance of new music was encouraged and promoted by groups like *Sentieri Selvaggi*, whose founder members include two composers, Filippo Del Corno (1970-) and Carlo Boccadoro (1963-). Their basic philosophy seems to suggest that 'contemporary' music at the turn of the new millennium should embrace a style that is both cross-cultural and multi-ethnic. The result is a highly accessible mixture of old and new, of intellectual and popular, of East and West. Del Corno's output ranges from meditative pieces such as the *Rifuggio intermedio* for harp and piano (1993), to more complex works like the Clarinet Concerto *Passage* (1997) or the more light-hearted *L'Uomo armato* (2000), the two latter works displaying his characteristic fondness for strongly syncopated rhythms. The energetic music of Boccadoro, too, is often suffused with the unmistakable rhythms of Latin American dance music, as implied for example in the title of his brief one-act opera *A qualcuno piace tango* (literally, 'Some people like tango' 1993).

In some cases the reference to modern dance music and pop culture has been much more blatant, and occasionally ironic. The decidedly cosmopolitan Lorenzo Ferrero (1951-) chose the pop icon Marilyn Monroe as the subject for his theatrical piece *Monroe* (1980) and five years later he included electric guitars in the score of his opera *Mare nostro* (1985), which contains several passages that borrow directly from the idiom of rock music. And towards the close of the century Andrea Liberovici (1962-) had the ingenious idea of setting various poems by Edoardo Sanguineti to a fashionable rap beat and recorded the result on a CD which he simply called *Rap* (1996).

The apparent ease with which composers like Liberovici appear to handle studio electronics highlights the fact that by the end of the century what had once been revolutionary was fast becoming commonplace – technology and attitudes had come a long way since the early experiments of Maderna and Berio. The extensive use of electronic resources soon became virtually indispensable in contemporary musical theatre. Berio's *Outis*, written in the mid-90s, calls for up to twenty loudspeakers distributed throughout the theatre, some on the stage and others variously located around the auditorium. And Corghi's opera *Tat'jana* (2000) typically combines live and recorded electronics, again broadcast from numerous speakers set up at strategic points around the theatre.

From the 1970s onwards composers and musicians were quick to take advantage of the growing number of courses in electronic music being offered by universities and conservatories. Claudio Ambrosini (1948 -), yet another prominent Venetian, was able to specialise in the subject at the Venice conservatory and went on to write numerous works combining traditional instruments with electronics. His *Satellite Sereno* (1990) makes use of a small instrumental ensemble backed up by live electronics and the name of the composition is a clear reference to Maderna's landmark piece *Serenata per un Satellite* written more than twenty years before.

Ambrosini's involvement with the experimental *Centro di Sonologia Computazionale* based at the University of Padua is just one example of how composers were now beginning to pool their ideas and to work in teams made up of musicians, computer technicians and sound engineers. The last quarter of the century saw the birth of various centres which soon became the focal point of research and experimentation in the field of electronics.

A particularly active role in the setting up of such institutions (and in the use of electronics in general) was played by Pietro Grossi (1917-2002), who despite belonging to a much older generation managed to remain at the forefront of technological developments until his death. In 1963 he founded the *Studio di fonologia musicale* in Florence and from 1965 taught on an innovative course specifically dedicated to electronic music at the Florence conservatory. He later moved to the *Centro Nazionale Universitario di Calcolo Elettronico* in Pisa where he continued his work and began to specialise in the creation of software packages for computer music. He subsequently branched into computer graphics and found an important outlet in the fastgrowing world of the internet.

Thanks to the groundwork carried out by specialists like Grossi, Florence soon became an important international centre for electronic research and experimentation. During the 1990s the importance of the city was further enhanced with the establishment of *Tempo Reale*, a centre for the promotion of contemporary music, which also dealt with the application of new technology in schools, an area very close to the heart of its director Luciano Berio. At the same time Milan re-established its status in the field of electronic music (which had dwindled a little after the closure of the *Studio di Fonologia della RAI* in 1983) with the formation of the new *Centro di Acustico ed Informatica Agon*, founded in 1990 by the composer Luca Francesconi (1956-), a former pupil of Stockhausen, Berio and Corghi.

Of the many younger composers who took full advantage of new technology special mention should be made of Fausto Romitelli (1961- 2004), a pupil of Donatoni and winner of numerous awards both at home and abroad. In many ways Romitelli's music could be said to draw together all the various strands of Italian postmodernism mentioned so far, combining, for example in a characteristic work like *En Trance* (1995), the natural sound of breathing with the mantra-like repetitions stemming from oriental philosophy, and elements taken from rock music.

Romitelli was fully aware of the fact that the rock revolution of the 1960s and '70s had irrevocably changed the way the general public listened to music, in particular helping them to grow accustomed to hearing electronically synthesized sound. He believed that the music of the rock era could not, and should not, be separated from the culture surrounding it. His three-part cycle *Professor Bad Trip* (1998-2000), for instance, explores the world of hallucinatory drugs and in doing so makes ostensive use of electric guitars alongside a more traditional chamber ensemble. But far from wanting to write a piece of rock music (in the words of the composer, the piece "unfortunately" still remains very much in the realms of *musica colta*), Romitelli tried to capture the essence of the genre, focusing on the repetitive riff-like nature of rock and using the electric guitars not so much to imitate the popular idiom, but rather to take advantage of the instrument's particularly 'raw' timbre. As such his exploration of primary sound (albeit with predominantly electronic means) has much in common with the work of Sciarrino, and his interest in exploiting limited ranges of pitch may even remind us of Scelsi. A direct line can therefore be seen between the earliest liberalising and minimalist tendencies of the '60s and '70s and the new brand of music being produced at the end of the century.

And yet against this background of technological advance and the increasing influence of popular culture, certain well-established themes remained remarkably unaffected. We have repeatedly underlined, for example, how the rediscovery of early music had been a continuous source of inspiration for Italian composers throughout the 20th century. The acknowledgement of this rich patrimony continued right up to and beyond the end of the millennium. Sciarrino, for instance, was fascinated with the figure of Gesualdo and among other things rearranged the madrigal *Tu m'uccidi o crudele*, substituting the keyboard accompaniment with a quartet of saxophones. Corghi was involved in the creation of new editions of works by Rossini and

Vivaldi; Ambrosini made transcriptions of music by Monteverdi; and Panni transcribed and re-elaborated works by Cavalli and Pergolesi, as well as looking to writers like Petrach for inspiration.

At the same time the importance of Verdi as a reformer not only of Italian opera but also of the very spirit of Italian music showed no signs of diminishing. Composers both young and old, revolutionary or reactionary, paid homage to their great progenitor by making reference to him and sometimes basing complete works on quotations from his works. The clear allusion to *La Traviata* in Donatoni's *Alfred, Alfred* and the reference to the march from *Aida* in Maderna's *Satyricon* have already been mentioned. Closer to the end of the century the well known slave's chorus from *Nabucco* gradually emerges during the course of Corghi's *La Cetra Sospesa* (1995), a cantata commissioned to mark the fiftieth anniversary of Italy's liberation at the end of World War II. And Vacchi's radio opera *La Burla Universale* (2001), written to commemorate the centenary of Verdi's death, owes its name and inspiration to the famous lines pronounced by Falstaff at the end of what was to be the venerable composer's last work for theatre: "*Tutto nel mondo è burla*".

While there is no doubt that the reforms carried out by Verdi in his maturity had pointed the way to a new and more flexible approach to opera writing, the traditional Italian melodrama, as we have already seen, was able to survive well into the second half of the century. The last truly lyric operas were probably written by composers like Menotti in the 1950s, but interest in the theatre as a medium for musical expression in a multitude of new and old forms continued to be as dynamic as ever. During the last two decades of the century composers like Marco Tutino (1954-) combined a straightforward narrative approach with a predominantly melodic style of writing that led to the huge success of his 'dramma concertante' *Vite Immaginarie* (1990), which was given more than 40 performances in its first season, an extraordinarily high number for a new opera at the time.

Vacchi too has tended to keep to a more or less conventional plot, for example in his 'French' operas *La Station Thermale* (1993-95) and *Les oiseaux de Passage* (1998), whereas other composers have taken on a distinctly more experimental approach. Sciarrino joined the ranks of Nono, Donatoni and Berio in writing what might be called an anti-opera, and preferred to describe his *Lohengrin* (1983-84) as an 'azione invisibile' rather than an opera, since the only apparent action comes from the images projected around the concert hall during the performance. The drama is almost entirely entrusted to a single singer who takes on the part of both main characters, Lohengrin and Elsa. And in his later work, *Luci Mie Traditrici* (1996), again inspired by Gesualdo, he virtually negates the traditional role of the orchestra by restricting its function to that of producing sounds that the characters react to on stage.

Sciarrino's work is just one example of the inevitable move towards economy of means that characterised opera writing during the closing years of the century. The need to cut costs eventually led to a proliferation of streamlined productions with smaller casts and less extravagance in general. Historically speaking, this tendency obviously owes much to the precedent set by Schoenberg with his monodrama *Erwartnung* but by the end of the century the small-scale opera was no longer a political statement but had become an economic necessity: suffice it to think of the unpretentious theatre pieces written in the 80s and 90s by Giorgio Battistelli (1953-), or Cardi's single act 'azione scenico-musicale' *Nessuna coincidenza* (1994-95). And even Clementi's complex yet hypnotic one-act opera *Carillon* (1991-92) is notable for its sparing use of resources.

On the other hand, another more recent Italian tradition, that of writing music for the cinema, was, and still is, positively thriving. A whole new wave of film-score writers followed in the well-trodden steps of Rota and Morricone. Some, like Vacchi and Einaudi, have made only occasional forays into the genre, but others have made it their speciality. The most successful of the latter category is undoubtedly Nicola Piovani (1946-) whose folk-tinged neo-romantic style has been used to good effect in his collaboration with some of the most notable Italian film directors of the second half of the century (including Bellocchio, Monicelli, Fellini, the Taviani brothers, Moretti and others). In 1999 his fame became truly international when his score for Roberto Begnini's *La Vita è Bella* (Life is Beautiful) won him an Oscar. And there has also been an increasing interest in supplying music for more alternative or experimental forms of cinema. Since 1991 Marco Dalpane (1956-) has made it his speciality to write and perform modern scores to accompany old silent movies (e.g. Guido Brignone's *Maciste all'inferno*), while Giovanna Marini has written evocative music to accompany the haunting and often denunciatory films of Gianikian and Ricci Lucchi.

As Italy finally moved towards the end of the millennium the feel-good factor that had brought cheer to the 1980s slowly began to wear off as people began to realise what really lay behind their country's miraculous economic growth. In 1992 the nation suddenly woke up to an enormous public debt and a grossly overvalued currency. The devaluation of the Italian Lira that followed had the effect of pushing up the cost of imported raw materials and slowing down an economy that had until then been the envy of the rest of Europe. Cuts in public

Ivan Fedele

spending had to be made and inevitably it was culture that bore the brunt of the reforms.

Organisers of music festivals and opera seasons were no longer inclined to risk alienating the general public by including too many unknown or 'difficult' items in their programmes. As a result several gifted but 'unproven' composers were forced either to live or at least to spend much of their time outside of Italy. The talents of Lorenzo Ferrero were, for example, first nurtured in Germany, not in his native Italy, while during the early 1990s Fausto Romitelli spent much of his time in Paris, where he could take advantage of the superbly equipped centre for electronic music IRCAM. And even the music of Scelsi and Sciarrino, as well as that of other established composers such as Luca Lombardi (1945-), Ivan Fedele (1953-) and Stefano Gervasoni (1962-), found a more welcoming audience abroad, a situation very reminiscent of that at the beginning of the century when the most innovative composers had discovered a more suitable climate for their creativity in countries like France and Germany.

Stefano Gervasoni

The shortage of money being channelled into music in general also led to a cutback in the number of national orchestras funded by the state. Until 1994 the national broadcasting company the RAI had boasted first-class orchestras in four different Italian cities (Turin, Rome, Naples and Milan), but sadly, due to a general lack of funds, they were all systematically disbanded and became fused into a single orchestra, known as the Orchestra Sinfonica Nazionale della Rai, based in Turin.

As far as Italy's grand opera houses were concerned, the century ended tragically. On 29 January 1996 the Teatro La Fenice in Venice was destroyed by a fire whose true origin still remains to be established. This sad incident occurred while the memory of a similar fate that had befallen the Teatro Petruzzelli in Bari (burnt down in 1991) was still fresh in people's minds.

Yet despite the apparent gloom there was still some room for optimism. At the turn of the new century the opening of two impressive new concert venues did much to restore the faith of the Italian people in their great musical tradition. The Milan Auditorium, a modern building designed to offer the best possible conditions for performers and audience alike, was inaugurated in October 1999 with a concert conducted by Riccardo Chailly. And three years later, in 2002, an even grander project was realised in Rome. The three concert halls making up the new Auditorium, strikingly designed by Renzo Piano, finally provided the capital with a modern centre for music making which until then it had lacked. The impressive list of guests invited to the grandiose inauguration ceremonies included the 97-year-old composer Petrassi, the grand old man of twentieth century Italian music who had lived through a century of turmoil but also of exciting innovation.

It seems fitting, then, to end this brief survey with the words of the Italian violinist Uto Ughi, who performed at the opening concert of the new Rome Auditorium: "I sincerely hope this marks the beginning of a new era for Italian music".

FURTHER READING

Many books have been written about Italian music in the modern era, but the vast majority focus almost exclusively on the well known composers of *opera lirica*. It would be a hard, if not impossible, task to suggest which of the many excellent biographies of Mascagni, Puccini etc. could be considered the most authorative. I shall therefore limit my suggestions to the literature covering the lesser known side of the story. As far as possible I have tried to refer to books written in English, but inevitably many of the more interesting titles are in Italian.

As a prelude to the 20th century, a lively portayal of Italian musical life in the 19th century can be found in John Rosselli's *Music & Musicians in Nineteenth-century Italy* (Amadeus Press, Portland 1991). Here readers will find references to composers like Martucci and Sgambati, as well as a detailed discussion on the plight of instrumental music in a country obsessed with opera. Moving into the 20th century, the social/economic situation is well covered in Martin Clark *Modern Italy 1871-1982* (Longman, London 1984, 1996), while R.J.B.Bosworth's *The Italian Dictatorship* (Arnold, London 1998) has a chapter devoted to music, film and literature.

Harvey Sachs gives a detailed account of how Italian composers and performers adapted to the requirements of the régime in his *Music in Fascist Italy* (W.W.Norton, New York 1988), but offers little in the way of musical examples. However, his well known biography *Toscanini*

(Weidenfeld & Nicolson, London 1978) takes us through the first half of the century in an interesting way and still remains a classic. A fuller picture of musical life under fascism can be found in Italian, in Fiamma Nicolodi's *Musica e Musicisti nel Ventennio Fascita* (Discanto, Fiesole 1984). Her book makes heavy reading, but persevering readers will find a wealth of facts and figures, as well as the occasional anecdote, for example about the meeting between the priest composer Perosi and Mussolini. It also contains a lengthy section documenting the historical correspondence between many composers and the Fascist authorities.

Most books dealing in general with twentieth century music contain brief references to the situation in Italy. For more a little more depth we must again turn to books written in Italian. The name that immediately springs to mind is Massimo Mila, a journalist and musicologist who was directly involved in the anti-fascist movement. His works include some very specific studies, such as an analysis of Petrassi's *Concerti per Orchestra*, but probably his best known book is the *Breve Storia della Musica* (Einaudi, Torino, 1963), which contains a chapter specifically dealing with contemporary music in Italy. A good description of the scenario towards the middle of the century can be found in Andrea Lanza, *Il Secondo Novecento* (E.D.T., Torino, 1980), while a more limited and less impartial view – but one that is nevertheless of great interest for its 'eye-witness' perspective – is available in Armando Gentilucci *Guida all'ascolto della musica contemporanea* (Feltrinelli, Milano, 1969).

Apart from the more familiar operatic composers, few Italians seem to have attracted full-blown biographies in English. Busoni has gained enough attention to merit what has now become a classic: E.J. Dent. *Ferruccio Busoni, a Biography* (OUP 1933, reprinted Eulenburg, London 1974, Da Capo Press, New York 1982). A book on Petrassi has been written in English, but was published in Italy: J.S. Weissman, *Goffredo Petrassi* (Edizioni Suvini Zerboni, Milan 1957, revised 1980), while Respighi, one of the best known Italian composers of the century, lacks a definitive English-language biography – although an abridged translation does exist of his wife's rather eulogistic account of his life:

Elsa Respighi, *Ottorino Respighi* (Ricordi, London 1962).

Books in Italian about the single composers mentioned in this book are surprisingly uncommon and more often than not consist of collections of essays and documents collected and edited by one or more authors. This is the case, for example, with M. Baroni and R. Dalmonte (eds.) *Bruno Maderna Documenti* (Suvini Zerboni, Milano 1985), which brings together a vast amount of documentation on Maderna and also includes an Introduction to his life and works. A similar approach is adopted in four important collections edited by Enzo Restagno: *Petrassi* (EDT, Torino 1986), *Nono* (ibid 1987), *Donatoni* (1990) and *Berio* (1995). Respighi is also given the same treatment in Giancarlo Rostirolla (ed), *Ottorini Respighi* (ERI, Torino 1985), a sumptuous collection of essays, letters, photos and paintings, with a fairly extensive section on his life. And Mario Ruffini *L'opera di Luigi Dallapiccola Catalogo Ragionato* (Edizioni Suvini Zerboni, Milano 2002) offers a complete catalogue of the works and writings of Dallapiccola, with an exhaustive analysis of each piece.

An interesting panoramic view of the musical climate in Rome during the years before and after the Second World War is offered in Carla Vasio's *Goffredo Petrassi Autoritratto* (Laterza, Bari-Roma 1991), literally a 'self-portrait' of Petrassi based on conversations with the composer. And finally, a very recent spate of interest in the genre of biography has led to the publication of several books, including Sergio Sablich *Dallapiccola* (L'Epos, Palermo 2004) and Graziella Merlatti *Lorenzo Perosi* (Ancora, Milano 2006).

As far as specific areas of interest are concerned, the work and activity of the Futurist composers is often mentioned in books covering Italian Futurism in general (i.e. dealing with Futurist Art and Literature). More details of the work and thoughts of Russolo can be found in G.F.Maffina *Luigi Russolo e l'arte dei Rumori* (Martano, Torino 1978). And a curious collection of essays and manuscripts pertaining to Pratella was compiled to mark the 40th anniversary of his death. The book, Domenico Tampieri (ed.) *Francesco Balilla Pratella* (Longo Editore, Ravenna 1995), also includes references to other contemporaries of Pratella (e.g. Casella and Malipiero) who briefly participated in the movement. For those interested in the underlying philosophy of the movement an English translation of the manifestos can be found in Umberto Apollonio (ed.) *Futurist manifestos* (trans. Caroline Tisdale, Thames & Hudson, London 1973).

A concise reconstruction of the progressive diffusion of serialism in Italy and elsewhere is offered in Roman Vlad's *Storia della dodecafonia* (Suvini Zerboni, Milano 1958). The history of electronic music, with special reference to Italy, is covered in A. Gentilucci *Introduzione alla Musica elettronica* (Feltrinelli, Milano 1972), while a detailed survey of the Darmstadt experience can be found in Antonio Trudu *La scuola diDarmstadt: I Fereinkurse dal 1946 a Oggi* (Ricordi, Milano 1992).

A great deal has been said and published about the San Remo festival, almost exclusively in Italian. However, an authorative article, including a technical analysis of the 'typical' San Remo song, has recently been written in English by Roberto Agostino: *Italian song and the Sanremo Festival. Change and continuity in Italian mainstream pop of the Sixties* (Popular Music, 26/3, 2007). The most complete book on the subject is probably Gianni Borgna, *L'Italia di Sanremo. Cinquant'anni di canzoni, cinquant'anni della nostra storia* (Mondadori, Milano 1998), while the Festival is placed in the general context of Italian popular music in Felice Liperi, *Storia della canzone italiana* (ERI-RAI Roma 1999). A more specific enquiry into the phenomenon of the Italian singer-songwriter is made in Paolo Jachia, *La canzone d'autore italiana 1958-1997* (Feltrinelli, Milano, 1998).

Finally, it should be added that a fair amount of literature, including biographies, historical accounts and essays, has been written and published in other languages, notably in French and German. Of particular interest are the monographic issues of the *Revue Musicale* (Richard Masse, Paris) dedicated to contemporary composers (eg. Luciano Berio, no. 375/377 1985) and the numerous studies and essays on the music of Luigi Nono written by Jurg Stenzl. However, to provide an exhaustive list of these publications is beyond the scope of the present book and readers are recommended to consult the Bibliographies following the relevant entries in Grove, or in the UTET *Dizionario della musica e dei musicisti*.

SELECTED BIBLIOGRAPHY

Basso, Alberto (ed) *Dizionario della musica e dei musicisti* (UTET, Torino 1994)

Lamarque, Lucio (ed) *Enciclopedia della Musica Garzanti* (Garzanti Editore, Milano 1999)

Lanza, Mario *Il Secondo Novecento* (E.D.T., Torino 1980)

Nicolodi, Fiamma *Musica e Musicisti nel Ventennio Fascita* (Discanto, Fiesole 1984)

Respighi, Elsa *Ottorino Respighi* (Ricordi, Milano 1954)

Rosselli, John *Music & Musicians in Nineteenth-century Italy* (Amadeus Press, Portland 1991)

Sachs, Harvey *Music in Fascist Italy* (W.W.Norton, New York 1988),

Sachs, Harvey *Toscanini* (Weidenfeld and Nicolson, London 1978)

Sadie, Stanley (ed) *The New Grove Dictionary of Music and Musicians* (Macmillan, London 2001)

Vasio, Carla *Goffredo Petrassi Autoritratto* (Laterza, Bari-Roma 1991)

Vlad, Roman *Storia della dodecafonia* (Suvini Zerboni, Milano 1958)

INDEX

128

Saint-Exupéry, Antoine de 80

Salviucci, Giovanni 77-78, 77 (photo)

San Remo (*see Festival di San Remo*)

Sangiorgi, Alfredo 105

Sanguineti, Edoardo 114, 130

Santoliquido, Francesco 43, 67

Satie, Erik 56, 57

Savinio, Alberto 57

Sbordoni, Alessandro 126-127

Scarlatti, Domenico 44, 56

Scelsi, Giacinto 16, 107-108, 109, 132, 136

Schaeffer, Pierre 99

Schafer, R. Murray 128

Scherchen, Herman 94

Schoenberg, Arnold 24, 46, 54, 66, 69, 73, 77, 81, 91, 92, 94, 105 (footnote), 117, 118, 134

Schoenberg, Nuria 94

Schubert, Franz 116

Schumann, Robert 35, 57

Sciarrino, Salvatore 127-128, 132, 134, 136

Sentieri Selvaggi 129

Serialism 8, 12, 14, 76, 78, 79, 80, 81, 84, 89, 91, 92, 94, 96, 98, 100, 102, 105, 108, 113, 117, 118, 119, 120, 122, 123, 124, 125, 126, 128

Setaccioli, Giacomo 16, 34

Settimana Musicale Senese 72

Sgambati, Giovanni 13, 32, 34, 43

Shakespeare, William 100

Sinatra, Frank 112

Sinigaglia, Leone 13, 36, 38, 70

Sinopoli, Giuseppe 124-125

Smereglia, Antonio 20, 43 (footnote)

Società Italiana di Musica Moderna 42, 53, 66

Solbiati, Alessandro 124, 124 (photo)

Sollima, Giovanni 129

Stockhausen, Karlheinz 14, 91, 92, 99, 102, 106, 131

Strauss, Richard 21 (footnote), 29, 35, 50, 88, 89

Stravinksy, Igor 24, 41, 42, 44, 46, 54, 55, 57, 72, 75, 77, 86, 104

Studio di fonologia della RAI 99, 114, 131

Studio di fonologia musicale, Florence 131

Tanglewood 86

Tartini, Giuseppe 46, 79

Taviani, Fratelli 134

Teatro a pannelli 53, 54, 116

Tebaldini, Giovanni 44, 48

Togni, Camillo 92, 93 (photo)

Tommasini, Vincenzo 43-44, 56

Toni, Alceo 8, 62-63, 65, 67, 69

Torchi, Luigi 44

Torrefranca, Fausto 45

Tosatti, Vieri 88, 109

Toscanini, Arturo 9, 14, 19, 21, 23, 25, 26, 34, 47 (footnote), 70, 71, 87